A Study on the Development of Women Entrepreneurs in Small Scale Industries

DR. I. PREM ROSE THAYAMMAL

Assistant Professor and Head

Department of P G Commerce

Jeyaraj Annapackiam College, Nallur

Tirunelveli District, Tamilnadu, India

PREFACE

"I Can Do All Things Through Christ Who Strengthens Me".

This research work entitled, A Study on the Development of Women Entrepreneurs in Small Scale Industries would have been impossible without the direct and indirect help and support of a number of important persons. I avail myself of this opportunity, with pleasure, to follow the good tradition of recognizing all those who, in one way or the other, contributed to make my study a success.

I praise **JESUS** for **HIS** sustaining grace that saw me through this thesis.

The project was undertaken in partial fulfillment of the requirements for the award of the degree of Doctor of Philosophy. The research was difficult, but conducting extensive investigation has allowed me to answer the question that we identified.

I would like to thank my supervisors for their excellent guidance and support during this process. I also wish to thank all of the respondents, without whose cooperation, I would not have been able to conduct this analysis.

To my other colleagues at my college: I would like to thank you for your wonderful cooperation as well. It was always helpful to bat ideas about my research around with you. I also benefitted from debating issues with my friends and family. If I ever lost interest, you kept me motivated. My parents deserve a particular note of thanks: your wise counsel and kind words have, as always, served me well.

I hope you enjoy your reading.

Dr. I. Prem Rose

CONTENTS

CHAPTER I

INTRODUCTION AND DESIGN OF THE STUDY

"When Women Move Forward; the Family Moves, the Village Moves and the Nation Moves".

- Jawaharlal Nehru

The world population has grown tremendously over the past two thousand years. In 1999, the world population passed the six billion marks. Latest official current world population estimate, for mid-year 2010, is estimated at 6,852,472,823. According to V.K. Singh and K.N Sudershan, the world population is growing at the rate of 97 million people per year and will touch 8.5 billion by the year 2025. About 95 per cent of the population growth will be in the developing countries. The Asian population is 3.55 billion, which may reach 4.54 billion by 2025 and women constitute around half of the total world population. As world economic profile of women shows, women represent 50 per cent of the world population, make up 30 per cent of the official labour force, perform 60 per cent of all working hours, receive 10 per cent of world income and own even less than one per cent of the world's property.

International Conference on Population and Development held in Cairo stressed on women empowerment and opined that a country's overall development and quality of people's life is more depended on women empowerment. In the words of the former President of India APJ Abdul Kalam, "empowering women is a prerequisite for creating a good nation, when women are empowered, society with stability is assured. Empowerment of women is essential as their thoughts and their value systems lead to development of a good family, good society and ultimately a good nation".

In advanced countries, there is a phenomenon of increase in the number of self-employed women after the World War II. In USA, women own 25 per cent of all businesses, even though their sales on an average are less than two-fifths of those of other small businesses. In Canada, one-third of small business is owned by women and in France, it is one-fifth.

In the era of liberalization, privatization and globalization along with ongoing information technology revolution, today's world is changing at a surprising pace. Political and economic transformations appear to be taking place everywhere as countries convert from command to demand economies, dictatorships move toward democratic system, and monarchies build new civil institutions. These changes have created economic opportunities for women who want to own and operate businesses.

At the same time 90 per cent of the rural women are unskilled and 88 per cent are illiterates which make them vulnerable to exploitation and economically dependent on men. No serious efforts have been made to improve the condition of women. There is a need to promote as entrepreneurship through which women of rural areas are empowered.

The word 'entrepreneur' is derived from the French word "Entreprendre" which means to undertake. In the early 16th Century it was applied to persons engaged in military expeditions, and was extended to cover construction and civil engineering activities in the 17th century, but during the 18th century, the word 'entrepreneur' was used to refer to economic activities. Many authors have defined 'entrepreneur' differently. Generally, an entrepreneur is a person who combines capital and labour for production. According to Cantillion, "An entrepreneur is the agent who buys means of production at certain prices, in order to sell at prices that are certain at the moment at which he commits himself to his cost".

Today, women entrepreneurs represent a group of women who have broken away from the beaten track and are exploring new avenues of economic participation. The reasons for women to run organized enterprises are their skill and knowledge, their talents, abilities and creativity in business and a compelling desire to do something positive. It is high time that countries rose to the challenge to create more support systems for encouraging more entrepreneurship amongst women.

Entrepreneurship development is a very crucial factor for the acceleration of economic growth of any country and the development of women entrepreneur is an essential part of human resource development. Women have started to show more interest in entrepreneurship because it provides them with the challenges they want to face and the chances of making more money. Moreover, technological development empowers women to acquire relevant qualifications and values to meet the demands of entrepreneurship.

1.1   Women Entrepreneurship in India

Women entrepreneurship development is an essential part of human resource development. The development of women entrepreneurship is very low in India, especially in the rural areas. Entrepreneurship amongst women has been a recent concern. Women have become aware of their existence, their rights and their work situation. However, women of middle class are not too eager to alter their roles in fear of social backlash. The progress is visible among upper class families in urban cities.

The Indian economy has been witnessing a drastic change since mid -1991, with new policies of economic liberalization, globalization and privatization initiated by the Indian government. India has great entrepreneurial potential.

In this dynamic world, women entrepreneurs play a vital role in the global quest for sustained economic development and social progress. Women have a unique position in the society. Real development cannot take place if it bypasses women, who not only represent one half of a country's population but also the kernels around which societal revolution takes place. Entrepreneurship enhances financial independence and self esteem of women. Around 50 per cent of India's population is women, yet business spheres such as trade, commerce and industry are still considered a male preserve. Entrepreneurial work has also been predominantly a man's world in India. Indian women are in no way inferior to men in any walk of life and they can be as good entrepreneurs as men. Therefore, it is essential to utilize the potential of Indian women.

Though women have played a key role in the Indian society, their entrepreneurial ability has not been properly tapped due to the lower status of women in the society. At present, women involvement in economic activities is marked by a low work participation rate, excessive concentration in the unorganized sector and employment in less skilled jobs. This is mainly because of the problems associated with their gender roles. Therefore, promotion of entrepreneurship and economic empowerment of women pose challenges to the government, funding agencies and non-government organizations. It is only from the Fifth Five Year Plan (1974-78) onwards that their role has been explicitly recognized with a marked shift in the approach from women welfare to women development and empowerment. Several policies and programmes are being implemented for the development of women entrepreneurship in India.

Women in India enter into business mainly for two types of factors i.e. pull and push factor. Pull factor refers to the process in which women are encouraged to start an occupation or venture with an urge to do something independently. Push factor refers to the process in which women are compelled to take up their own business in order to tackle their economic difficulties. In India, most of the women now show their preferences towards the entrepreneurship rather than going into the fields of professional or other services. Women choose both the traditional (toy making, pickle making, candle making, etc.) as well as the non-traditional (running garment shops, beauty-parlours, computer-centres, etc.) activities and they perform well. Generally, women opt for micro-enterprises because of certain unavoidable factors and issues like, limited capacity, low level of confidence, little access to technical information, poor local market conditions, less access to capital, etc.

1.2   Present Status of Women Entrepreneurs in India

Since the 21st century, the status of women in India has been changing as a result of mounting industrialization and urbanization and social legislation. Over the years, a large number of women are going in for higher education, technical and professional education and there is a considerable increase in the number of women in the work spot. With the spread of education and awareness, women have shifted from the kitchen, handicrafts and traditional cottage industries to non-traditional higher levels of activities. The Government has also laid special weightage on the requirement for conducting special entrepreneurial training programms for women to enable them to start their own ventures. Financial institutions and banks have also set up particular cells to help women entrepreneurs. This has rebound the women entrepreneurs on the economic scene in the recent years although many women entrepreneurship enterprises have still remained a much neglected field. Bharati Kollan and Indira J Parikh analyze the status of women rightly comment, "For women there are quite a lot of handicaps to enter into and manage business ownership due to the intensely entrenched conventional state of mind and strict principles of the Indian society".

1.3   Successful Leading Business Women in India

The 21 Leading Businesswomen in India are

1.   Akhila Srinivasan, Managing Director, Shriram Investments Ltd.
2.   Chanda Kocchar, Executive Director, ICICI Bank
3.   Ekta Kapoor, Creative Director, Balaji Telefilms
4.   Jyoit Naik, President, Lijjat Papad
5.   Kiran Mazumdar-Shaw, Chairman and Managing Director, Biocon
6.   Lalita D Gupte, Joint Managing Director, ICICI Bank
7.   Naina Lal Kidwai, Deputy CEO, HSBC
8.   Preetha Reddy, Managing Director, Apollo Hospitals
9.   Priya Paul, Chairman, Apeejay Park Hotels
10.   Rajshree Pathy, Chairman, Rajshree Sugars and Chemicals Ltd
11.   Ranjana Kumar, Chairman, NABARD
12.   Ravina Raj Kohli, Media Personality and ex-President, STAR News
13.   Renuka Ramnath, CEO, ICICI Ventures
14.   Ritu Kumar, Fashion Designer
15.   Ritu Nanda, CEO, Escolife
16.   Shahnaz Hussain, CEO, Shahnaz Herbals
17.   Sharan Apparao, Proprietor, Apparao Galleries
18.   Simone Tata, Chairman, Trent Ltd
19.   Sulajja Firodia Motwani, Joint MD, Kinetic Engineering
20.   Tarjani Vakil, former Chairman and Managing Director, EXIM Bank
21.   Zia Mody, Senior Partner, AZB & Partners

1.4   Role of Women as Entrepreneurs

Considering the flow of women entrepreneurs in the traditional industries, it was often criticized that the women entrepreneurship are engaged only in handloom and handicraft enterprises. But now their career has been broaden into new line like hotel lines. In the last decade, there has been a remarkable shift from the traditional industry to non-traditional industry and services. Based on this concept, some important opportunities are being identified, considering the socio-economic, cultural and educational status and motivational level of women entrepreneurs, particularly projects with low investment, low technical know how and assured market are suggested for them such as production of soaps, detergents, ready made instant food products including pickles, spices, incense stick making, candle making, papad, manufacturing of woolen goods, beauty parlour business, typing centre, xeroxing, job contracts for packaging of goods and distribution and household provision etc.

1.5   Categories of Women Entrepreneurs

The women entrepreneurs are classified into three categories based on the woman entrepreneur's role in management of the enterprise: (1) Women-Managed Units (WMU), (2) Jointly Managed Units (JMU) and (3) Men-Managed Units (MMU). WMUs were those units, which strictly come under the description of a woman enterprise under WIP (Women Industries Programme). These units are owned and managed by women and 80 per cent of the employers are women. JMUs are units in which women have 50 per cent control all aspects of management and at least 50 per cent of the employment goes to women. MMUs are, on the other hand, women's enterprises only in name, the dejure 'entrepreneur' not even knowing much about the enterprise and playing little or no role in management irrespective of whether the employees are women or not.

1.6   Women Entrepreneurs and Their Constraints

Life for woman entrepreneurs having a small scale industry is not a bed of roses.   The individual woman entrepreneur single-handedly faces a plethora of seemingly endless problems.

1. Bank and other financial institutions do not consider middle class women entrepreneurs as serious applicants for setting up their projects and they are hesitant to provide financial assistance to unmarried women or young girls because it is not clear who will return the loan either parents or in-laws. This humiliates unmarried women and they generally leave the idea of setting up their ventures.

2. The attitude of the officers of the support system is neither motivating nor encouraging, as they are under the impression that setting up of business or industry is not the women's cup of tea.

3. Financial support system suffers from unpredictable delays.

4. Moving in and around the market, is again a tough job for middle class women entrepreneurs in Indian social system.

5. Women cannot get registered sales tax number without a male partner. This again humiliates prospective women entrepreneurs.

6. The security or surety and collateral requirements of the banks and financial institutions frustrate unmarried women and young girls. It is extremely difficult for young girls particularly those coming from a lower socio-economic level to set up a modest sized unit as their own financial and other resources are barely inadequate to meet the promoter's contribution.

7. Men in the role of father, brother or husband, in general, are not ready to accept entrepreneurship as career option for women in their homes, as it is a full time activity and ultimately prevents them from doing their household duties.

8. It has been impressed in the minds of women that for married middle class women in India, family is the priority and for unmarried women, marriage is the priority because of Indian social system.

An International Labour Organization (ILO) report on women entrepreneurship identifies the following problems faced by women entrepreneurs.

1. Lack of family support: Family members make the women feel guilty of neglecting their household duties in their pursuit of business obligations. Cultural traditions hold back women from venturing into their own businesses.

2. Lack of capital: Traditional sources of finance like banks are reluctant to sanction loan to women entrepreneurs if they do not have any male or family backing. This is especially true of lower income women.

3. Lack of confidence and faith: Lack of role models undermines the self confidence of women entrepreneurs. The activity of selling is considered abhorrent to the female gender.

4. Lack of right public and private institutions: Most public and private incentives are misused and do not reach the women unless they are backed by men. Also many trade associations like ministries, chambers of commerce do not cater to women expecting women's organizations to do the necessary thing.

While analyzing the problems faced by women entrepreneurs in India, Kirve and Kanitkar conclude, "women, who try to play the entrepreneurial role, generally have to face the environmental constraints. There are the chances for having high rate of failure for the one who is starting a business at the cost of her own effort and risk. Thus, this rate of loss might go even higher in the case of women who have to face the business, family and social problems. Consider the case of the highest literate state where the women are getting the full chance of showing their skills and proficiency. Such an environment is beneficial and suitable for the growth and development of women entrepreneurs".

1.7 Schemes for the Development and Promotion of Women Entrepreneurs

According to the Third All India Census of Small Scale Industries conducted in 2001-02 and subsequent estimates made, only 10.11 per cent of the Micro and Small Enterprises in India are owned by women while 9.46 per cent of the MSE (Medium Scale Enterprises) are managed by women. In 2006-07; it is estimated that 12.99 lakh women managed enterprise and 12.15 lakh women managed enterprise.

In order to encourage more women enterprises in the MSE sector, several schemes have been formulated by this Ministry and some more are in the process of being finalized, targeting only at the development of women enterprises in India.

1.7.1 Trade Related Entrepreneurship Assistance and Development Scheme for Women (TREAD)

With a view to encourage women in setting up their own ventures, government implements a scheme, namely, Trade Related Entrepreneurship Assistance and Development (TREAD) during the Eleventh Plan. The scheme envisages economic empowerment of women through the development of their entrepreneurial skills in nonfarm activities. There are three major components of the scheme:

1. Grants up to 30 per cent of the total project cost are given to the Non-Government Organizations (NGOs) for promoting entrepreneurship among women. The remaining 70 per cent of the project cost is financed by the lending agency as loan for undertaking activities as envisaged in the project.

2. Grants up to Rs1 lakh per programme is given to training institutions or NGOs for imparting training to the women entrepreneurs, subject to these institutions or NGOs bring their share to the extent of minimum 25 per cent of grant and 10 per cent in case of NER.

3. Need-based grants up to Rs5 lakh is given to National Entrepreneurship Development Institutions and any other institution of repute for undertaking field surveys, research studies, evaluation studies, designing of training modules etc.

Operationalisation of the Scheme

The scheme envisages that women associations, NGOs and SHGs should prepare composite bankable proposals for a group of women entrepreneurs, and submit to the office of the DC (MSME) for forwarding to the banks for their appraisal. The banks examine the proposal and issue the approval. 30 per cent of the loan amount is sanctioned as grant and made available to the bank by the office of DC (MSME) for further disbursement to NGOs.

1.7.2 Micro & Small Enterprises Cluster Development Programme

Existing Clusters

A cluster is defined as a group of enterprises, ideally having 100 members, producing similar products or services. While 100 members could be the minimum per cluster, depending on the density of population and other factors, even 200-300 could be a good target group for undertaking diagnostic study and the subsequent Soft Interventions in a cluster. However, in difficult and backward regions the target numbers could come down to 50 or less but it should not be too small as a lot of Government expenditure is made per cluster. The Cluster Development Programme

(CDP) being implemented envisages diagnostic study of identified clusters of traditional skill-based MSEs to identify appropriate technologies and their providers and to facilitate adoption of available technology meeting the specific needs of the end users. The cluster development aims at enhanced competitiveness, technology improvement, adoption of best manufacturing practices, marketing of products, employment generation etc.

Type of interventions

A. Soft Interventions: They are capacity building activities in the cluster where no fixed assets is acquired or formed. Soft interventions, inter alia, include

1. Diagnostic study
2. Forming Association-Trust building and Developing Identity
3. Capacity building
4. Organizing workshops and seminars
5. Training and Exposure visits
6. Market development
7. Launch of Website
8. Common procurement
9. Common or complementary sales and branding

In the past, depending upon the type of cluster, assistance available for soft interventions varied in the range of Rs25 – Rs35 lakh per cluster. Currently we have an internal ceiling of Rs10 lakh for soft intervention under this scheme.

B. Hard Interventions: Hard interventions, inter alia, include

1. Setting up of Common Facility Centres (CFCs),
2. Mini Tool Room
3. Design Centre
4. Testing Facilities
5. Training Centre
6. R & D Centre
7. Common Raw Material Bank/Sales Depot
8. Display/Exhibition Centre

In case of the hard intervention, the contribution from the M/o MSME varies between 30 and 80 per cent of the total project cost, but in the case of clusters owned and managed by women entrepreneurs, contribution of the M/o MSME could be up to 90 per cent of the project cost.

Creation of Infrastructure

This Ministry implemented the IID Scheme to provide developed sites with infrastructural facilities like power distribution network, water, telecommunications, drainage and pollution control facilities, roads, exhibition/display centre, raw materials, storage and marketing outlets, common service facilities and technological back-up services, etc. This scheme has been subsumed in the MSME-Cluster Development Programme. All the features of IID Scheme have been retained.

To create physical infrastructure exclusively for women enterprises central grant of 40 per cent of the project cost subject to a maximum of Rs2 crore is available. The Ministry of MSME is making efforts to enhance the quantum of grant to 80 per cent in a project of Rs10 crore.

Operationalisation of the Scheme

1. A Cluster Development Executive (CDE) is required for executing and monitoring all soft interventions in a cluster. Normally, a CDE can be a DIC Officer/MSME-DI officer/retired expert or even hired person from Non-Government Sector.

2. The hard interventions in a cluster and creation of physical infrastructure require setting up a user's body/special purpose vehicle which could be society/trust/company to be formed by the cluster beneficiaries.

1.7.3 Credit Guarantee Fund Scheme for Micro and Small Enterprises

This scheme was launched in August 2000 to ensure better flow of credit to micro and small enterprises by minimizing the risk perception of financial institutions and banks in lending without collateral security. Under this scheme, guarantee cover is provided to collateral free credit facility extended by Member Lending Institutions (MLIs) to the new as well as existing micro and small enterprises on loans up to Rs50 lakh. The guarantee cover available is up to 75 per cent of the loans extended. The extent of guarantee cover is 80 per cent for (i) micro enterprises for loans up to Rs5 lakh; (ii) MSEs operated and/or owned by women; and (iii) all loans in the North-East region. The lending institutions availing guarantee from the Trust have to pay one time guarantee fee of 1.5 per cent and service charges of 0.75 per cent per annum of the credit facility sanctioned. For loans up to Rs5 lakh, the one time guarantee fee is 1 per cent and service charges are 0.5 per cent per annum of the credit facility sanctioned.

1.7.4 Support for Entrepreneurial and Managerial Development

MSME-DIs regularly organize a number of Entrepreneurship Skill Development Programme (ESDPs)/ Entrepreneurship Development Programme (EDPs)/ Management Development Programmes (MDPs) to train the potential entrepreneurs in improving their techno/managerial knowledge and skill with a view to facilitating them to start MSEs in various fields.

Many of the programmes are tailor made for the target group for SC, ST, OBC, Women, Minorities and other weaker sections. These programmes are also called "Out-reach Programmes" as they are conducted in rural / less developed areas.

22.5 per cent of total target of ESDPs/EDPs are conducted exclusively for SC, ST, Women and Physically Challenged persons with a stipend of Rs500 pre months per candidate under the promotional packages for MSEs. No fees are charged for SC, ST, woman, and physically handicapped.

1.7.5 Exhibitions for Women under Promotional Package for Micro & Small Enterprises Approved by CCEA under Marketing Support

DC (MSME) has formulated a scheme for women entrepreneurs to encourage Small & Micro manufacturing units owned by women and register in DI/DIC in their efforts at tapping and developing overseas markets, to increase participation of representatives of small/micro manufacturing enterprises under MSME stall at International Trade Fairs/Exhibitions, to enhance export from such units. Under this scheme, participation of women entrepreneurs in 25 international exhibitions is envisaged during the Eleventh Plan (2007-2012).

With a view to encourage women entrepreneurs to participate in the International Exhibitions under MDA scheme it has been decided to

1. provide rent free space (6/9 Sq Mts) in the exhibitions
2. reimburse 100 per cent economy class air fare for one representative
3. the overall ceiling shall however be Rs1.25 lakh.

1.8 Programmes and Organizations for the Development of Women Entrepreneurship in India

The government of India and state government of Tamil Nadu have introduced a number of schemes for the development of women entrepreneurs. The development schemes are implemented with the help of government organization and non governmental organization for the benefit of women entrepreneurs. The followings are the Programmes and Organizations:

- Entrepreneurship Development Programmes (EDPs)
- Development Programmes of Central Social Welfare Board
- Rural Industries Programme of SIDBI
- Prime Minister's Rozgar Yojana (PMRY)
- Micro Credit Scheme
- Mahila Samakhya Project (MSP)
- National Policy for the Empowerment of Women
- Indira Mahila Yojana (IMY)
- Women's Component Plan (WCP)
- Swarna Jayanti Shahari Rozgar Yojana (SJSRY)
- Technology Development & Utilisation Programme for Women (TDUPW)
- Swa-Shakti Project
- Trade Related Entrepreneurship Assistance and Development of Women (TREAD)
- Swarnajayanti Gram Swarozgar Yojana (SGSY)
- Revised Scheme of TREAD
- Scheme of Assistance to Women Co-operatives
- Schemes of National Bank for Agriculture and Rural Development (NABARD)

- National Entrepreneurship Development Board (NEDB) Scheme
- Schemes of Consortium of Women Entrepreneurs of India (CWEI)
- HUL-Shakti project of Hindustan Unilever Limited
- Centre for Entrepreneurship Development
- Schemes of Small Industries Development Bank of India (SIDBI)
- Women Enterprise Development Scheme (WEDS) of North Eastern Financial Institution
- Schemes of State Bank of India
- Schemes of Punjab National Bank
- Schemes of Canara Bank
- Schemes of Dena Bank
- Scheme of Bank of India
- Scheme of Union Bank of India
- Schemes of Central Bank of India
- Scheme of Orient Bank of Commerce

1.9   Women Entrepreneurship in Small Scale Industries (SSI)

Small Scale Industries play a key role in the industrialization of the country. It is considered as an important means for checking concentration of economic power in a few hands and bringing about economic dispersal and more equitable distribution of national income. The nature and characters of SSI are suitable for women to become entrepreneurs.

Women entrepreneurs are a woman or a group of women who initiate, organize and operate a business enterprise. The government of India considers the enterprise of women entrepreneurs as "an enterprise owned and controlled by women saving a minimum financial interest of 51 per cent of the capital and giving at least 51 per cent of the employment generated in the enterprise to women".

The small-scale industrial units are functioning in all the states in India. According to the third All India Census of Small Scale Industries, there are 10.52 million units functioning in India. The total employment contribution of the sector is 24.93 million, with a per unit contribution of 2.37. The state of Utter Pradesh tops the list with more than 17 lakh SSI units followed by Andhra Pradesh, Maharashtra,

Madhya Pradesh and Tamil Nadu. Sikkim has the lowest number of small scale units (368 units).

In India, small scale industrial units are owned both by men and women. Among the small scale industrial units owned by women entrepreneurs in India, Kerala tops the list with 1.39 lakh units, followed by Tamil Nadu with 1.30 lakh units. Tamil Nadu ranks second in the total number of small-scale units owned by women entrepreneurs in India. Lakshadweep has the lowest number of small-scale units owned by women entrepreneurs (67 units).

Among the 94.57 lakhs SSI units owned by men functioning in India, 86.92 per cent are unregistered and registered units amount to 13.08 per cent. In the total number of SSI units owned by men functioning in India more than four-fifths of the units (86.92 per cent) are unregistered. In 10.64 lakhs SSI units owned by women, 87.07 per cent units are unregistered and 12.93 per cent units are registered. More than four-fifths of SSI units (87.07 per cent) owned by women are unregistered.

1.10   Statement of the Problem

Presently women entrepreneurs comprise of 10 per cent of the total entrepreneurs in India. It is also clear that this percentage is growing every year. The role of women entrepreneurs helps to solve the problems of unemployment and poverty. Development of women entrepreneurs is an essential part of human resource development. Entrepreneurship amongst women has been a recent concern. The development of women entrepreneurs is very low in India, especially in the Tirunelveli District.

Several government entrepreneurial programmes and schemes focus on women in small scale industries. Propounded by different departments and initiated at different times, most of the schemes share a lot of common features. The Women Industries Programme (WIP) offers 50 per cent subsidy limited to Rs25,000 for building construction and machinery for the business under the small scale industries. Entrepreneurs are offered free Management Training Programmes and stipend during the training period in small scale industries. Subsidies are given to women entrepreneur in the small-scale industries sector; the Khadi and Village Industries Commission

(KVIC) gives 30 per cent margin money as subsidy (limited to Rs10 Lakh) as against the 25 per cent for the general category. Irrespective of these special incentives, women enterprises encounter several problems. Often, women are merely fronts for men to obtain concessional credit, subsidies, and other incentives offered for women enterprises. Duplication of the same type of enterprises (herd mentality) is rampant among women units, limiting themselves to certain limited areas of work. Many women units do not opt for business expansion even when they have scope for it. To top it all about 90 per cent of the women units are reported to be sick.

Reports by government departments and financial institutions have mentioned about constraints imposed on women entrepreneurs in small scale industries by their immediate environment, such as family commitments and absence of appropriate psychological disposition on the part of women themselves. However, the primary focus of attention of policy makers still remains on constraints such as lack of short-term and long-term credit facilities. Similarly, conventional training programmes are organized on general management areas such as production, finance, and marketing personnel on the assumption that these are the main skills required for successful entrepreneurship. However, these do not seem to be the sole or even the most important factors. The outcome of various Entrepreneurship Development Programmes (EDP) shows that even when credit is provided, women hesitate to set up units or if they set up units, they do not succeed in their ventures.

The banking sectors also play a vital role for the development of women entrepreneurs in India. Several nationalized banks in India have special schemes for promoting entrepreneurship, especially enterprises owned by women. The state and central government also organize many training programs for women entrepreneurs through the banking sectors. But low awareness and a passive mindset ensure that there are very few takers. Though a number of credit schemes are available for women, there are several bottlenecks as well. There are some barriers between banking sectors and women entrepreneurs so that the bank schemes have not reached the women entrepreneurs.

Rajesh Kumar Shastri and Avanika Sinha have reported in their study that women's entrepreneurship needs to be studied separately for two main reasons. The first reason is that women's entrepreneurship has been recognized during the last decade as an important untapped source of economic growth. Women entrepreneurs create new jobs for themselves and others and also by being different. They also provide the society with different solutions to management, organization and business problems as well as to the utilization of entrepreneurial opportunities. The second reason is that the topic of women in entrepreneurship has been largely neglected both in society in general and in the social sciences. Not only have women lower participation rates in entrepreneurship than men but they also generally choose to start and manage firms in different industries than men tend to do.

Although the significance of these factors is recognized, systematic studies on them do not exist, partly due to the difficulties of conducting such studies and partly to the fact that policy conclusions are not immediately obvious since the process of changing these factors will take time. Nevertheless, given the fact that there is a large financial outlay on the part of the government which has spent huge amounts on women development programmes, but with limited success, the role of these factors in inhibiting women's entrepreneurial growth demands serious enquiry, particularly in Tirunelveli District with the advent of local level planning and proliferation of new schemes modeled on the old pattern.

In view of the above situation, the researcher decided to take this study to identify the development of women entrepreneurs. The present study aims to analyze the factors of various developments, constraints and perception on banking sectors of women entrepreneurs in Small Scale Industries in the district. The results of the study would serve as a guidepost for the development of the women entrepreneurs in Small Scale Industries in the area where the study has been undertaken.

1.11 Objectives of the Study

The overall objective is to analyze the development of women entrepreneurs in Small Scale Industries in Tirunelveli district. The specific objectives of the study are:

1. To study the profile and background of the respondents.

2. To study the organizational profile of enterprise of the respondents.

3. To analyze the various developments on personality, social, personal, innovational, embankment and intellectual of the respondents.

4. To analyze the various constraints faced by the women entrepreneurs to run their enterprise.

5. To study the overall perception of the respondents on banking sector.

6. To offer suitable suggestions based on the findings.

1.12 Null Hypotheses

To give a specific focus to the objectives, null hypotheses have been formed to test the objectives on clear terms using appropriate statistical tools. It necessitates the development of hypotheses at each and every stage of the analysis. The study involves 15 hypotheses which are listed down, proved and explained in detail in the fourth, fifth and sixth chapters. The following is the list of hypotheses formulated for the study.

1. There is no significant development on the selected variables of women entrepreneurs compared to the average level (Mean = 10)

2. There is no significant Personality Development in all categories of women entrepreneurs.

3. There is no significant Social Development in all categories of women entrepreneurs.

4. There is no significant Personal Development in all categories of women entrepreneurs.

5. There is no significant Innovational Development in all categories of women entrepreneurs.

6. There is no significant Embankment Development in all categories of women entrepreneurs.

7. There is no significant Intellectual Development in all categories of women entrepreneurs.

8. There is no significant difference among Mean Rank of development variables of Factor – Personality Development.

9.   There is no significant difference among Mean Rank of development variables of Factor – Social Development.

10.   There is no significant difference among Mean Rank of development variables of Factor – Personal Development.

11.   There is no significant difference among Mean Rank of development variables of Factor – Innovational Development.

12.   There is no significant difference among Mean Rank of development variables of Factor – Embankment Development.

13.   There is no significant difference among Mean Rank of development variables of Factor – Intellectual Development.

14.   There is no significant difference among Mean Rank of Development Factors of Women Entrepreneurs.

15.   There is no significant difference among Mean Rank variables of Constraints of Women Entrepreneurs.

1.13   Methodology

The methodology adopted in the present study includes the selection of the study area, the research design, the sampling technique, the collection of data, the period of study and tools of analysis.

1.13.1 Selection of the Study Area

The industrial growth of a district is conditioned by natural resources, infrastructural facilities, transport and technical know how. These have helped building up industries in the district of Tirunelveli. Tirunelveli district has been endowed with several facilities for the rapid growth of women entrepreneurs when compared to other districts in Tamil Nadu but unfortunately it is one of the industrially backward areas in the state. Tirunelveli district is the native district for the researcher. These are the main reasons for selecting Tirunelveli district as the study area to analyze the developments of women entrepreneurs in Small Scale Industries.

1.13.2 Research Design

Research design is the arrangement of conditions for collection and analysis of data, in a manner, that aims to combine relevance to the research purpose, with economy in procedure.

In the present study, Observational designs and Ex-post-facto research design was followed. Singh (1980) defined Ex-post-facto research as a design that draws the influences regarding the relationship between variables on the basis of such independent variables whose manifestations have already occurred. Del Siegle (2009) explained the causal comparative (ex post facto) research that the groups are already formed. It does not meet the standards of an experiment because the independent variable in not manipulated. The researcher has no control over the independent variables because they occurred much prior to her research effort.

1.13.3 Sampling Technique

Snowball sampling, which is considered a form of accidental sampling, is adopted for the present study. According to Allen Rubin and Earl R. Babbie, snowball sampling is appropriate when the members of a special population are difficult to locate. The term snowball refers to the process of accumulation as each located subject suggests other subjects. The sampling procedure also results in samples that have questionable representativeness, so it is used primarily for exploratory purposes. Nevertheless, snowball sampling is an important and commonly used technique in qualitative research, and in research on minority and oppressed population it is often necessary

In order to study the developments of women entrepreneurs in small scale industries in Tirunelveli district, 380 women entrepreneurs in small scale industries and services were identified as sample evenly from 19 blocks of the district by adopting the snowball sampling technique. In Tirunelveli district, women entrepreneurs are emerging in various fields namely Petty Shop, Tailoring, Garment, Handicrafts, Beauty Parlour, Catering Services, Dairy Farming, Poultry, Job Works (Typing, Xerox, Lamination, Computer Centre, STD/ISD booth, etc.) and the like. Since most of the women entrepreneurs are running small-scale units, the data regarding the number of women entrepreneurs are not available in the government departments. Hence raw data were obtained from 380 women entrepreneurs who were identified by snowball sampling techniques. From each of the 19 blocks of the district, 20 women entrepreneurs were selected which comes to a total of 380 respondents for this study.

1.13.4 Collection of Data

The present study was based on both primary and secondary data. Well structured and pretested interview schedule was used for collecting primary data by personal interview method. The interview schedule was prepared by a five-point Likert scale to collect the information required for the study after an in-depth review of the previous studies related to the topic of the present study, discussions with the officials of the District Industries Centre (DIC) and experienced women entrepreneurs in Small Scale Industries. It was then judged for content validity and pre-tested on a group of conveniently selected respondents to assess its clarity and ease of completion. Based on the recommendations received, it is modified and subsequently given to the study sample for the data collection. The interview schedule focuses on six development factors, women centered constraints and perception of women entrepreneurs on banking service. In the interview schedule, some questions consist of multiple items while others are single items.

Secondary data have been collected from books, journals, newspapers, periodicals, reports, internet, unpublished Ph.D theses, and unpublished records of District Industries Centre, Tirunelveli. The data from directorate of industries and commerce, Chennai and Tamil Nadu Industrial Investment Corporation Ltd. have also been collected in their websites.

1.13.5 Period of Study

The study was conducted in the year 2010 – 11. The primary data were collected from the women entrepreneurs in small scale industries and services during the period from March 2010 to January 2011. The data related to the developments of women entrepreneurs were obtained from the date of starting their enterprises.

1.13.6 Tools and Techniques of Data Analysis

Descriptive analysis has been used to analyze the profile and background of women entrepreneurs, organizational profile of enterprise and to draw inferences. In the descriptive analysis, the sample units were divided into three, based on the woman entrepreneur's role in management of the enterprise into (1) Women Managed Units (WMU), (2) Jointly Managed Units (JMU) and (3) Men Managed Units (MMU) for the purpose of the analysis.

The development of women entrepreneurs on various variables and the development of three categories of women entrepreneurs were assessed by using the One-Sample t Test procedure. In order to find out the significant development of women entrepreneurs on various variables, the constant test value (Average mean value = 10) was used.

In order to analyze the development factors such as personality development, social development, personal development, innovational development, embankment development and intellectual development of women entrepreneurs, Factor Analysis has been administered. In Factor Analysis, the Kaiser-Meyer-Olkin was used to find out the sampling adequacy, Bartlett's Test was used to find out the sphercity, Principal Component Analysis Method was used to find out the significant development of the factors and Varimax of Orthogonal Rotations Method was used to find out the loadings of the variables on the factors. Correlation Matrix was used to find out the degree of relationship of variables on one and each other. Friedman Test has been used to find out the significant difference between the true mean variables of development factors and also between the factors. If the Friedman Test result was statistically significant then Wilcoxon Signed-Rank Tests was used as post-hoc test to examine where the differences actually occur.

In order to find out the loadings of various constraints of women entrepreneurs to run their business, Varimax of Orthogonal Rotations Method in Factor Analysis has been administered and Friedman Test has been used to find out the significant difference between the true mean constraints of women entrepreneurs. Descriptive and GAP Analysis has been used to find out the perception of women entrepreneurs on banking service and the gaps between the women entrepreneurs and the banking sector.

Data cleaning began at the end of each day and the data were entered into the computer. Advanced statistical analyses of the study were performed using significant statistical software, like SPSS. Before analyzing the data, the editing of the data were again done by using software. After the analysis, the data were interpreted on the basis of analytical results. Before applying statistical tools, the data were tested for normality i.e. Non-Parametric Test namely Kolmogorov-Smirnov Tests.

1.14 Significance of the Study

The research in women entrepreneurs is providing new insights and innovation to the women entrepreneurs as well as to the policy makers in enterprises. The ultimate goal of research in women entrepreneurs is to help women to develop their enterprises and improve their performance based on new concepts. The findings of this study will be of significance in many fields and the results of the study may

1. add to the existing fund of knowledge with regard to the development of women entrepreneurs in small scale industries.

2. provide guidelines, which will help the District Industries Centre (DIC) and committed NGOs in preparing the training programmes and schemes for women entrepreneurs in small scale industries.

3. help the government and policy makers in enterprises to find out the cluster of enterprises sector and sick area of enterprises for women entrepreneurs in small scale industries.

4. help the government and policy makers in enterprises to find out the constraints of women entrepreneurs to run their enterprises.

5. help the bank officials to remove the gaps between banking service and women entrepreneurs.

1.15 Limitations of the Study

1. The study covered only Tirunelveli district. Hence the findings and conclusions of the study are entirely applicable to this district only and it may not hold good for other areas.

2. The study was based on the perceptions of the women entrepreneurs, whose attitudes may change with the change of times. Therefore, the responses reflect only their contemporary views on the prevailing conditions.

3. Present study covered only the women entrepreneurs engaged in manufacturing and service sector under Small Scale Industries.

4. Data collection through interview schedule was a time consuming matter. The respondents sometimes were found non-cooperative with the interviewer.

5. Further, it was also found that women entrepreneurs had a tendency to reveal their income as low and expenses as high thinking that this would help them to get more credit.

1.16   Scheme of Work

The present study, "A Study on the Development of Women Entrepreneurs in Small Scale Industries in Tirunelveli District" has been organized under seven chapters.

The first chapter includes details related to women entrepreneurs in India, present status of women entrepreneurs in India, role of women as entrepreneur, women entrepreneurs and their constraints, categories of women entrepreneurs, the schemes, programmes and organizations for the development of women entrepreneurs in India and women entrepreneurs in small scale industries. Besides, the statement of the problem, objectives, methodology, limitations and scheme of work has been presented.

The second chapter is about the reviews of the past studies related to the present study. Further, it discusses the concepts used in the present study.

The third chapter describes the profile of the study area and the profile of the small scale industries in Tamilnadu and Tirunelveli District.

The fourth chapter deals with the analysis and interpretations of the personal profile and the organizational profile of the enterprise of the respondents.

The fifth chapter enlists the analysis and interpretations of developments on various variables and factors such as Personality Development, Social Development, Personal Development, Innovational Development, Embankment Development and Intellectual Development of the respondents.

The sixth chapter deals with the analysis and interpretations of various constraints and overall perception on banking service of the respondents.

The seventh chapter presents the summary of findings along with the conclusions and suggestions based on the analysis done.

CHAPTER II

REVIEW OF LITERATURE

This chapter presents the review of literature of the past research studies and the concepts used in the present study. Though a large volume of literature is available on the subject of the development of women entrepreneurs in small scale industries, only a few important studies have been reviewed here. Such a review would facilitate the researcher to have a comprehensive knowledge of the concepts used in the earlier studies and would enable the researcher to adopt, modify and formulate an improved conceptual framework for the use of the present study with a view to drawing meaningful conclusions.

2.1 Review of Literature

Abdul Moyeen and Afreen Haq (1994) have analyzed the various problems faced by the urban female entrepreneurs of the Dhaka Metropolitan area in their article. They studied 51 female entrepreneurs in respect of the nature of their business management skills, level of education, occupational influences, and demographic information. Their study revealed that the mean age of women entrepreneurs lies between 25 and 40 years. Seventy per cent of the samples were married with children. Sixty per cent attended college or University of whom 27 per cent had Masters' Degree. Their parents were more educated than the general people and 73 per cent of the women entrepreneurs belonged to the upper or upper middle class. The majority of women entrepreneurs' husbands had business background and 20 per cent of the female entrepreneurs were actively assisted by their husbands. Over 90 per cent of the samples were engaged in the service sector. Only 3 per cent were engaged in manufacturing, 55 per cent of the enterprises were partnership type while 45 per cent were sole ownership type, 60 per cent of the enterprises had been in operation for only five years or less. 60 per cent of these female-managed enterprises had only one to three employees, most of whom were women. The organizational structures were informal. Most of them had no formal training and so they lacked managerial skill needed to run business enterprises. They also faced financial problems during the startup stage. Many of them talked about their personal problems.

Abu Saleh (1995) in his article "A Profile of the Women Entrepreneurship in Bangladesh" tried to discern the motivation of women entrepreneurs for entering into business and assessed the entrepreneurial skills of the women entrepreneurs. He also tried to evaluate the performance of women entrepreneurs in their business. The study showed that the training the women entrepreneurs received was theoretical and 80 per cent of the sample had no business background or experience. Only 15 per cent had business experience varying from 5 to 15 years. Only 5 per cent had experience in the same type of business and 90 per cent of women entrepreneurs came to business on their own initiative. Only 10 per cent of the women had acquired business through inheritance. The study also showed that the majority of women entrepreneurs (60 per cent) were engaged in production i.e. manufacturing and 25 per cent were engaged in the service sector and 15 per cent in trading. About 45 per cent women employed workers on fulltime basis and 10 per cent did manage their business without outside workers. The average number of persons employed was 14.

Aida Idris (2008) attempted to generate a profile of innovative women entrepreneurs based on their personal and business characteristics. Data were compiled from a sample of 138 women entrepreneurs in Peninsular Malaysia, and analyzed using ANOVA to determine any correlation between the independent and dependent variables. He found out that women's entrepreneurial innovativeness was very much affected by their age and education, as well as the type, location and size of business.

Andrea E. Smith-Hunter and Swithina Mboko (2009) analyzed the strategy processes employed by Zimbabwean female small business owners, and established the link between the strategy processes and firm outcome. They used interviews to collect data, using a case study method approach, which directed the interview process. Based on their macro analysis, they concluded that Zimbabwean female business owners have strong entrepreneurial competence but lack the ability and support to develop their firms to their full potential.

Asha Das (1998) in "Women in Business" elucidated that the Government has launched training programmes exclusively for self employment of women through schemes such as support for training and Employment Programme of Women (STEP), setting up of training cum employment cum production units (NORAD), and

Development of Women and Children in Rural areas (DWCRA). It has also ensured that in other general schemes 30-40 per cent of the benefits are embarked for women as in the case of training of rural youth for self employment and integrated rural development programme. Government programmes and initiatives are meant to act as catalysts and establish the capacity, potential and suitability of women as entrepreneurs and encourage private and public sectors to open greater avenues for them.

B. Subrahmanyeswari, K. Veeraraghava Reddy and B. Sudhakar Rao (2007) investigated on Entrepreneurial behaviour of rural women farmers in dairying. A multidimensional analysis was conducted by following ex-post facto research design and random sampling technique in Chittoor district of Andhra Pradesh. A total of 120 respondents comprising of 61 small, 35 medium and 24 large rural women farmers in dairying were selected by proportionate random sampling technique. The results revealed that majority of the dairywomen farmers possessed medium entrepreneurial behaviour and variation among the three categories of the respondents was found to be significant. Entrepreneurial behaviour was positively and significantly related with land holding, material possession, management orientation, value orientation, income from dairy farming, education and innovativeness.

Bandana Saha (2007) dealt with the general problems faced by women entrepreneurs in their business development. Finance was identified as the main problem of the women entrepreneurs. The author found that the women entrepreneurs of Dhaka City were all educated and 43 per cent of them had post-graduate degrees. Most of them belonged to families with business background. They had easy access to technology, finance, market and packaging facilities. The women entrepreneurs were engaged in readymade garments, embroidery, herbal medicine and food products like dry fish, pickles etc.

Bharti Kollan and Indira J. Parikh (2005) analyzed the development and status of the women entrepreneurs in their study. They concluded that women have become aware of their existence their rights and their work situation. However, women of the middle class were not too eager to alter their role in fear of social backlash. The progress was more visible among upper class families in urban cities. The study enthused from the era of fifties to the 21st centuries and how transformation has occurred in the women roles. Also the study explained the status of women entrepreneurs and the problems faced by them when they ventured out to carve their own niche in the competitive world of business environment.

Bhatia, Saini and Dhameja (1999) in "Women Entrepreneurs – their perception, about business opportunities and attitudes towards entrepreneurial support agencies (A study of Haryana state)" revealed that women are entering the field of entrepreneurship in increasing numbers and they do so in the face of many obstacles. Despite numerous barriers, they demonstrate a strong determination to succeed. They contribute to bring prosperity to themselves, their families and to the economy in general. Business ownership provides women with the independence they crave for. The society also needs to undergo an attitudinal change with regard to the role of woman as entrepreneur.

C. Rani (1992) mentioned that there is a significant association among economic status and the time spent towards managing the enterprise as well as on training. The high and middle income groups received a better training compared to low-income group since the low-income groups are not aware of the importance of training.

C. Rani (1997) opined that the participation of women in economic activity is a must for the development of the country. At present, the rate of participation of women is very low; only 28 per cent of them are working women and the percentage of self employed women is only 5.7 per cent. The percentage of women entrepreneurs is found to be only 6.7 out of the 16 million SSI entrepreneurs in India.

C.H. Aravinda and S. Renuka (2002) identified the important factors which motivated women towards entrepreneurship in their study. The facilitating factors that had an impact on maintaining the enterprises successfully were self-experience, interest, family's help and support. Women entrepreneurs, in general, face conflicts in their roles in work place and home. The main conflict in work role pertains to inability to expand the enterprise by optimum utilization of available skills.

Carter and Rosa (2002) identified in their study that the female entrepreneurs tended to write more and respond in ways that suggest that they tend to reflect more upon the future and new possibilities. Differences in style of operations were evident.

Others have reported in the study that written responses from female entrepreneurs described in greater detail and more clearly the urging need for governmental support of networking activities and other programmes that promote co-operation and resource pooling.

Colette Dumas (2001) studied on the Centre for Women and Enterprise Community Entrepreneurs Programme (CEP). This case analysis was an attempt to determine the initial outcomes of the community entrepreneurship programme. He indicated that training provided to low-income women has indeed accomplished its goals—to help participants launch their own businesses, to empower them to achieve self-sufficiency through entrepreneurship and to advance the economic health of Boston's inner city neighborhoods through micro enterprise and job creation.

D. P. Moore and E. H. Buttner (1997) suggested that women started their own businesses from a desire for self-determination and for career challenge, and that they expected the corresponding respect, recognition, and self esteem that both self-determination and challenge provide. Primarily, entrepreneurship is a survival instinct that motivates women to start a business. Around the world, dismal economic conditions, high unemployment rates, and divorce catapult women into entrepreneurial activities. Desperate to put food on the table for their children, women are defying societal norms in order to survive.

Dafna Kariv (2008) investigated the relationship between entrepreneurs' stress-appraised as positive or negative and their business's financial performance, i.e., turnover of men owned businesses (MOB) and women owned businesses (WOB). The results, culled from the responses of 190 Israeli entrepreneurs, indicated that men and women appraise stress differently—predominant stressors for women were negligible for men and vice versa. A hierarchical regression emerged that positive stress triggers the business's turnover and negative stress impedes it; interactions of gender with social support and role conflict augmented the simple effects of each stressor alone on business turnover.

Dill Bagh Kaun, M. Annadurai and V.K.Sharma, (2003) concluded that besides providing technical and financial assistance, it is essential to educate rural women and extend entrepreneurial management and marketing skills so as to enhance their confidence and competence so that they would become self reliant.

Gounaris, Stathakopoulos and Athanassopoulos (2003) in their study dealt with the measurement of service quality of banks in India. It investigates the discrepancy between customers' expectations and perceptions towards the quality of services. The study was conducted using the SERVQUAL instrument. The results indicate that the sample population has perpetual problems with their banking service experiences. Findings from this study provide initial direction in determining the optimum service quality attributes to focus on in promoting banking services.

Hala Wasef Hattab (2010) investigated the relationship between the external environmental factors and the growth of female entrepreneurial projects, through evaluating the factors of growth: annual increase in the number of projects, development of projects' activities, and the increase in project size (capital, number of employees and expansion). He concluded that there was a significant impact of the dimensions of technological environment on the growth of entrepreneurial projects.

J.B. Bilesanmi-Awoderu and O.O. Kalesanwo (2009) discussed how Universal Basic Education (UBE) programme could be used to promote women entrepreneurship in science and technology with the resultant effect of enhancing female scientists' participation in national development in Nigeria. They have established the militating factors against women scientists' entrepreneurship in Nigeria. They pointed out the factors, suggestions for encouraging and promoting women scientists' entrepreneurship such as encouragement of female education in science and technology, socio-cultural perspectives, proper networking of successful women in science and technology in order to serve as mentor to others.

James Kimo Williams (2010) analyzed the gender-based attributes and challenges in the music industries in his study. His emphasis was women continue to struggle in this male-dominated industry and must develop a different set of entrepreneurial tools to take advantage of industry opportunities. He asserted that the music industry has moved to a more interactive environment in which women can better manage their art or business and not have to compromise their artistic aesthetic or cater to gender-driven attitudes to find success.

Jill R. Kickul, et.al., (2007) examined the influence of formal and informal social capital and training needs of 421 women entrepreneurs that the acquisition of financial resources needed for growth. They pointed out that women entrepreneurs with high growth resources tended to use more formal social networks and needed training in strategic planning and production/operations.

Jitendra Ahirrao and Sadavarte (2010) found in their study that dual role of women is the major constraint of women entrepreneurs followed by prejudice against women, male domination, lack of economic freedom, absence of family encouragement, problems of public relation, lack of exposure, no risk bearing capacity, lack of self-confidence and fear of social security. Out of the total respondents, the highest number of entrepreneurs did not have any knowledge of finance or the procedure of loan taking from the banks. They hesitated to go to the banks for inquiry about the loan for their businesses.

Johnson and Storey (1993) made a comparison between men and women entrepreneur in their study and concluded that women entrepreneurs were older than men, less competent in their occupation, less successful in obtaining capital from banks and they had higher ratio of partnership.

K. Thangamani and V. Uma Priya (2001) identified that 56 per cent women obtained a profit of Rs 500/- and below 34 per cent of women gained Rs 501 - Rs 1000. Only 10 per cent of women had a profit of Rs 1,001- Rs 1,500. In total, 88 per cent of the women expressed that they had gained profit from their enterprises. Out of this, fifty six per cent women obtained a profit of Rs 500/- and below. It was found that sixty two per cent utilized the profit, for the expansion of business by investing more on the purchase of raw materials whereas 24 per cent women utilized the profit for the family expenditure followed by 14 per cent utilizing the profit for the education of their children.

K.Sivalognathan (2002) pointed out that the problems faced by women entrepreneurs in India are inequality, family background, low wages, inadequate training, government policies, exploitation by middlemen, problem of finance, scarcity of raw-materials, stiff-competition, high cost of production, low mobility, social attitudes, low ability to bear risk, lack of education, low need for achievement, project related problems, family ties, shortage of power, inadequate infrastructure facilities and socio economic constraints.

K.V. Irniraya (1999) in "Development of SSI Sector and Women Entrepreneurs: Role of Central Government" revealed that with the help of policy initiatives, incentives and facilities by the Government of India, the small scale sector will continue to grow at a faster rate facing the challenges posed by liberalization and globalization and contribute substantially to the Indian economy. Since women entrepreneurs also constituted an inseparable segment of SSI sector, promotion and empowerment of women entrepreneurs was implicit in the expectation.

K.V. Nagarajan and Elaine G. Porter (2005) studied women entrepreneurs' experiences in terms of their motives and the obstacles they faced in establishing and growing their businesses. They covered nine women entrepreneurs in a small southern Indian town with entrepreneurial training and who had been running in their business for at least five years were part of a focus group. They found out that work-family conflicts were among them. Women used gender-based strategies to manage interactions with governmental and bank officials and a professional demeanor to deal with male clients. Children sometimes participated in their businesses after school.

Kalyani and Chandralekha (2002) observed that the socio-economic and demographic characteristics have a significant impact on the involvement of women entrepreneurs, particularly when it comes to enterprise management. Many of them received help from their family members, particularly the male members, in carrying out various kinds of work.

Kamar Jahan and Veerasekaran (2000) found out that the women entrepreneurs in Tamilnadu engaged in three important activities namely manufacturing, trade and commerce and services. Manufacturing includes food-based and cloth-based products. The trade and commerce activity include retail trade in food items, fruits, vegetables, flowers, etc. Services include community, social and personal repair services like beauty parlour, tailoring, money lending and pawn broking, etc.

Katar Singh and Raji Gain (2002) pointed out that the women distributed their work in three shifts. In the mornings, a team of four women prepared cows for milking and undertook distribution of milk, recording of milk yield and clearing the shed. The second team of three in the afternoon prepared feed, washed the utensils and made dung cakes. In the evenings the third team of three women milked the cows, distributed the milk and recorded the yield. The shifts were taken up by rotation. The total expenses and total income were equally shared by the women.

Katerina Sarri and Anna Trihopoulou (2005) investigated the issue of women entrepreneurs in Greece by looking into personal characteristics and motivation of female Greek entrepreneurs. They covered the period of 1990-2000. They emphasized those women entrepreneurs are not treated as a monolithic category: rather, policies and programs to support them should begin with a diagnosis of their personal characteristics and motives aimed at strengthening pull motives that comprise a base for more viable and innovative entrepreneurial activity.

Kaza P. Geetha (1997) investigated why banks were not able to meet their targets for women enterprises in Baroda. He also found the over-riding importance of family for women and instances such as marriage, childbirth or even a crisis in the family led to closure of enterprises of women. He pointed out that financial institutions were therefore hesitant to give loans to women entrepreneurs as they might quit even a well-running business for the sake of their families. This factor also led women to locate their enterprise near their homes even if it meant compromising on business interests.

Kyaruzi Imani Silver and Hales Chantal Ahoefa (2009) examined the processes of incubating African female entrepreneurs in their study. They focused on current understanding of the nature of the complex processes of providing business support services to female entrepreneurs in Africa, an analysis of how incubation might address those challenges, and some tentative lessons drawn from their empirical research and entrepreneurs` own experiences. They collected data from 160 in Dares Salaam, Tanzania firms and 40 female-owned businesses in Dakar, Senegal. They pointed out that the specific circumstances of female-owned businesses failed or succeeded in the competitive business environment, which was often dominated by men. They concluded that African female entrepreneurs were constrained by structural, cultural and institutional barriers; the solutions to overcoming such barriers remained problematic. Also, their roles in the incubation processes were rarely mentioned in most policies on entrepreneurship in Africa.

Lalitha Rani (2000) identified the two major problems faced by the women entrepreneurs to be dual career and wrong evaluation of the product by the customers. Securing financial aid and marketing had also been listed as other issues which posed a problem for the women entrepreneurs. Derogatory comments by their husbands and relatives and negative criticism by the immediate society were the societal barriers for women entrepreneurs.

Laquita C. Blockson, Jeffrey Robinson and Sammie Robinson, (2007) in his study "Alleviating Poverty through Business Ownership: Personal and Professional Success Experienced by African American Women Entrepreneurs" found out that these women defined entrepreneurial success for themselves in a multitude of ways, using both economic/financial indicators and non-economic/non-financial indicators. They believed their rich experiences – particularly given their status as minority entrepreneurs, women entrepreneurs, and entrepreneurs of growth firms – might provide evidence that could help shape an augmented definition for entrepreneurial success.

Lucy Sendi and Alistair R. Anderson, (2007) investigated the nature of micro finance, or micro credit, in rural Tanzania. They began by examining the types of finance available to the poor who operated micro enterprises. Based on their macro analysis, they concluded that most institutes which offered loan facilities operated mainly in urban centre, thus restricting accessibility for the rural poor. Moreover, the modest lending conditions also created an obstacle for the poorest women. They also concluded that self loans have had some benefits in improving the profitability of micro enterprises run by rural poor women, but there seemed to be little long–term effect as measured by increases in household assets.

Makararavy, Anurit, Pacapol, Walsh and John, (2009) identified the challenges and opportunities faced by the women in a high context culture such as Cambodia. An examination by the researchers revealed that women entrepreneurs faced distinctive challenges in the early part of SME development in terms of social problems, marketing problems, lack of government assistance and financial problems.

Mallika Das (2007) examined the problems which women faced during the setting up and continued operation of their businesses, and the work-family conflicts. The study also looked at their reasons for starting a business and the self-reported reasons for their success. It covered the two states in southern India- Tamil Nadu and Kerala. He found that the initial problems faced by these women seemed similar to those faced by women in western countries. However, Indian women entrepreneurs faced lower levels of work-family conflicts and seemed to differ in their reasons for starting and succeeding in business.

Manimekalai (2002) mentioned that the entrepreneurship was not confined to any particular stratum of society, sex or race and that there was There is no difference between men and women on the basis of personality recognition. However, entrepreneurial women still constituted only a small percentage of the total self-employed population in the developing countries. Majority of them had low initial investment and 100 per cent of the investment was made out of their own effort. The major problems faced by these women were lack of funds for initial investment, lack of knowledge of procedures for acquiring loans, non-implementation of existing policies, etc.

Manuela Pardo-del-Val (2010) in his study, "Services Supporting Female Entrepreneurs" pointed out that many public initiatives act as fund services which support women entrepreneurship. The study took a closer look at the characteristics of female entrepreneurs, their motivations, and the difficulties they face in their ventures. The researcher concluded that policies for the support of women entrepreneurs should aim at strengthening pull motivators and concentrate in designing programmes specifically tailored to the type of business, focusing on long-term policies rather than short-term initiatives.

Masuda M. Rashid Chowdhury (2002) made an attempt in her article to identify some of the factors that led to the adoption of women entrepreneurship. She also discussed the problems faced by the women entrepreneurs in their business enterprises.

As small entrepreneurs, women played a significant role in the national economy. In the article, she suggested that the governmental and non-governmental development for women entrepreneurship should be activated in order to increase the contribution of women towards the national economy. She also rightly identified the major problem of women entrepreneurship which included the lack of credit facilities, skill training, market opportunities, difficulties in procurement of raw materials and transportation. She also pointed out that some middlemen created problems by offering low prices.

Mathur and Anamika (1987) found that men and women did not differ significantly with regard to innovative trait and internal focus of control. They also found that women were in no way inferior to men in terms of intelligence, foresight, curiosity and healthy.

Muhammad Azam Roomi and Guy Parrott (2008) investigated a study on Barriers to Development and Progression of Women Entrepreneurs in Pakistan. They pointed out that the economic potential of female entrepreneurs was not being realized as they suffered from lack of access to capital, land, business premises, information technology, training and agency assistance. They also observed the inherent attitudes of a patriarchal society that held the view that men were superior to women and that women were best suited to be homemakers, and were not created to face challenges. In progression side, women received little encouragement from some male family members, resulting in limited spatial mobility and a dearth of social capital.

Munira Sestic (2009) did a comparative study on the increased willingness of starting their own business of Bosnia women and that of Herzegovina women and also their turnover from the 20th the 21st century. He pointed out the current state of unemployment of women, as well as their educational structure depended mainly on their choice of starting their own business. Alongside he listed the reasons why a number of women were not ready to start their own.

N. Rajani (2008) examined the quality of micro-enterprise management by women in socio-cultural milieu and projected the management training needs of women entrepreneurs. She concluded that confidence building, competence, connections and capital were projected as essential management training needs for women entrepreneurs.

Neelaveni, Rambabu, and Venkata Ramaiah, (2000) found that age factor, mass media consumption, and extension contact were significantly influencing the variation in developmental priorities of farm women in agri- business management. Age was found to be significantly and negatively associated with developmental priorities. As age increased, their energy declined and hence their attention in management of activities in agri-business declined. As mass media consumption and extension contact increased, their exposure to new technologies in agri-business management increased thereby increasing their attention in management of agri-business activities.

Pijush Kanti Chowdhury and Begum Nurun Nahar (2005) in their article "Women Entrepreneurs of Rural Industries in Some Selected Areas" made an attempt to (i) identify the factors responsible for emergence of rural women as entrepreneurs, (ii) assess the socio-economic impact of entrepreneurship on their lives and living and (iii) assess the problems faced by the women entrepreneurs in their business. The authors observed that illiterate and less educated women preferred bamboo and cane-work and other crafts like sewing, garments making and embroidery. Seventy-Nine per cent of the sample became entrepreneurs due to circumstances that compelled them to find out some source of income for their living. It was also found that the majority of women entrepreneurs (76.47 per cent) acquired initial experience about the craft either from families or from neighbours.

Pillai and Anna (1990) made an attempt to study women entrepreneurship in Kerala. Their objective was to find the social, political, and economic factors that prevented entrepreneurship development. A randomly selected sample of 102 women entrepreneurs in the Ernakulam-Kochi area was surveyed. The study showed that entrepreneurs depended on financial support from the State and that familial assistance was used only as a secondary source of help. Yet, women had cited family support and encouragement as the highest facilitating factors for them to do business.

Pooja Nayyar, et.al., (2007) concluded in their study that women entrepreneurs faced constraints in aspects of financial, marketing, production, work place facility and health problems. The financial problems faced were non-availability of long-term finance, regular and frequent need of working capital. Poor location of shop and lack of transport facility were major marketing problems. Production problems included the problem of non-availability of raw material. Entrepreneurs of zone-IV mainly faced health problems such as fatigue, tension, and headache. Women entrepreneurs also faced problem of improper water and space facility. Guidelines framed as a solution to these problems can help women entrepreneurs to deal with these problems effectively.

Prabakaran and Satya (2003) examined the various service attributes in the banking sector and the study pointed out that the borrowers were not only satisfied with the money they got as loan; they were also keen about how they got it. Quality Service alone would act as winning edge in the highly competitive environment where there was not much of product differential. Quality service was exhibited in the study through the dimensions namely reliability, tangibility, responsiveness, assurance and empathy.

R. Ganesan, Dilbagh Kaur and R.C. Maheshwari, (2002) studied the problems, confronted by the self-motivated women entrepreneurs, and then highlighted the prospects and the future challenges. They identified the concern areas of these women who were in business and also proposed what kind of entrepreneurial training would be ideal.

R. Hisrich and C.G. Brush (1982) found that female entrepreneurs proved to be visionaries and catalysts, whereas male entrepreneurs were more traditionalists. Female entrepreneurs tended to place more of an emphasis on the balance of important life factors in measuring success.

R. Magesh, (2010) studied the service quality and its model of gaps were studied by taking the service offered by the banks into account. Gap analysis was used as an analytical approach for evaluating the difference between customers' expectations and the experience of quality. He conclude that, though the satisfaction level of service being offered was at an acceptable level, the organization had to keep abreast in an ever changing environment to be competent and bridging the gap between the customers' experience and expectations. By identifying strengths and weaknesses pertaining to the dimensions of service quality, organizations could allocate better resources to provide better service.

Rani D. Lalitha (1996) examined the socio-economic background of women entrepreneurs, analyzing their motivational factors, major strengths and weaknesses against their environmental threats and opportunities. She also investigated the degree of work-home conflict and its effects on enterprise performance. The sample of 100 entrepreneurs showed that women entrepreneurs belonged mostly to nuclear families. Irrespective of the fact that they had supportive families and husbands which made home management easy, the women seemed to give priority to their families rather than to their enterprises. They tended to prefer micro-enterprises as they could be managed together with discharge of their domestic responsibilities. Such factors forced women to make compromises even when the environment offered opportunities for growth and diversification. Irrespective of family structure, number of children, and economic status of the family, the work-home conflict was found to be present.

Rolanda P. Farringtone Pollard (2006) determined the relationship between women entrepreneurs' support and success from both actual and perceptual perspectives. He found out that women's motivations toward entrepreneurship were strongly correlated with perceptions of success and that women's perceptions of success were highly correlated with their perceptions of support.

S.Mythili (2003) concluded that the successful women entrepreneurs became inspiration to others. They could become big industrialists and participate in global economy. They could help raw charity trusts and patronize them. The social inequalities were mitigated by keeping a good relationship with the surroundings.

Sadrul Huda, Sayeed Alam and Yunus Khan (2009) conducted a comparative study on women entrepreneurs. They found out that woman in informal and formal sector started business for independence. In both sectors the size of the business was small and operated from their residence. With successful business performance most of the women in formal and informal sectors wanted to extend the business. There was no significant difference between women owned business in formal and informal sector. The size of the business, ease of entry and cost of doing business were same in both the sectors. Women in formal sector did not receive enough support from the authority.

Sandberg (2003) revealed that doing business in rural sectors seemed to diminish gender–related barriers. He obtained that it was advantageous for women to start business in rural areas, where inhabitants seemed to be more concerned with economic opportunity than gender distinctions. Quality gender difference was that female owners and operators were more articulate than their male counterparts. As a result, they were better in describing the problems common to both males and females.

Sanjukta Mishra (2009) investigated the status of women entrepreneurs and the problems faced by them when they ventured out to carve their own niche in the competitive world of business environment. He found that women in India faced many problems to go ahead in business. The greatest deterrent to women entrepreneurs was that they are women. The financial institutions were skeptical about the entrepreneurial abilities of women. The male-female competition was another factor, which developed hurdles to women entrepreneurs in the business management process.

Sayeed and Nusrat (2008) found that the most frequent barriers faced by women entrepreneurs were lack of difficult to get help from the financial institution, obtaining trade license, tax certificate etc. Other barriers are absence of proper women business community to raise the issue to the policy makers of the country, absence of business training institution to teach them how to start the business.

Selvamalar and Ayadurai (2005) examined the constraints faced by women entrepreneurs, the challenges they faced, and the entrepreneurial ventures they had established over the past three decades in a war-torn area - the northeast of Sri Lanka. They collected the data only from the Tamil women of Sri Lanka, even though the greater majority was the "Singhala" women. They concluded that the constraints that had been found to be similar in the northeast and the other Asian and African countries were: i) lack of financing and funding; ii) balancing time between the entrepreneurial venture and family; iii) poor access to education and training programmes to help women improve their entrepreneurship, managerial and technical skills; and iv) inefficient production systems and weak infrastructure. They also concluded that the biggest constraint was lack of international aid which was however not seen as a major problem in many of the other Asian and African countries.

Shailendra Singh and Saxena (2000) revealed that the women entrepreneurs of eastern U.P. struggled against many odds namely traditional culture, low economic opportunity, low special accessibility and the personal characteristics namely shyness, lack of achievement, motivation, low risk-taking, low education level, unsupportive family environment, lack of information and experience, problem of liquidity and finance.

Shiva Malik and Taranjit Kaur Rao (2008) conducted an empirical study among 135 women entrepreneurs in Chandigarh to analyze the reasons for starting business, perception regarding their success in business and quality attributed to their success. The study revealed that women were ready to face the challenges associated with setting up of business. Papad, pickles were the things of the past, now with new and innovative business, women entrepreneurs were fast becoming a force to reckon with in the business world. Women were not into business for survival but to satisfy their inner urge of creativity and to prove their capabilities. Women education was contributing to a great extent to the social transformation.

Sindhu S. Narayan and P.S. Geethakutty (2003) pointed out that entrepreneurship had been recognized as an essential ingredient of economic development. Very high literacy rate and lack of employment opportunities paved way for many unemployed youth including women to take up small-scale business units. In their study, entrepreneurial success index (ESI) was developed to measure the level of success of women in agribusiness and the respondents were classified into four groups of very high success, high success, medium success and low success.

Su Fei Lim, Kathryn Smith and Colin Bottomley (2003) investigated the incidence of and success of those female entrepreneurs who graduated from university and at some point in their careers opted for establishing their own business ventures in Scotland. They reported their initial findings of that work, which was based on a series of intensive and in-depth interviews with a number of Scottish graduate female entrepreneurs. Through these interviews interesting revelations emerged which contributed to the better understanding of the success factors, such as gender-related motivation for business start-ups and the importance of gender networking to the graduate female entrepreneurs. They found out that the female graduate entrepreneurs received no specific entrepreneurship education during their higher education studies. This paper concluded with recommendations that might serve to ensure that graduate female talent should be retained within the Scottish economy and should not "escape" from Scotland to pursue careers elsewhere. Policymakers, economic development agencies and universities should see to it that Scotland must retain its graduate talent in order that continuing economic revival could be sustained.

Sunday Samson (2009) investigated the influence of psychological capital on women entrepreneurs' innovative behaviour with 405 female entrepreneurs from Ibadan, Nigeria. The result indicated that women with high self-efficacy and internal locus of control scored higher on entrepreneurial innovative behaviour than women with low self-efficacy and external locus of control. There was also a significant relationship between highly educated women and lowly educated women. Women were encouraged to believe in themselves while their acquisition of higher education will provide impetus for growth and achievement in entrepreneurial innovative activities.

Surapa Raju's (2000) study revealed that the pull category of women entrepreneurs was younger than the push category entrepreneurs. Most of the pull category women were of upper castes and majority of the push category belonged to backward class and Scheduled class categories. After starting the enterprises, the average monthly income of the pull and push entrepreneurs increased by 4.0 and 1.2 times respectively. The percentage contribution of push entrepreneurs' income to their family income is nearly 69 per cent whereas in the case of pull category it is only 34 per cent.

T.J. Kamalanathan and V. Vijaya, (1996) in "Perceptions and Environmental Concerns of Potential Women Entrepreneurs" revealed that entrepreneurs were the harbingers of economic growth and were the backboned of many technological and industrial innovations. The policies they adopted, with regard to waste management from their production processes were a crucial determinants of the status of the environment.

Tulus Tambunan (2009) examined recent developments of women entrepreneurship in Asian developing countries in his study. It focused only on women entrepreneurs in small and medium enterprises. The findings of the study showed three main important facts. First, SMEs were of overwhelming importance in the region, as they account, on average per country, for more than 95 per cent of all firms in all sectors. Second, the representation of women entrepreneurs was still relatively low which could be attributed to factors such as low level of education, lack of capital, and cultural or religious constraints. Third, most of the women entrepreneurs in SMEs were from the category of "forced" entrepreneurs seeking for better family incomes.

Uddin Sami and Ziauddin Khairoowala (1989) concluded in their study that in developing countries women entrepreneurs faced considerable repercussions within their families and social relationships because of the role transformation from that of the traditional homemaker to a business person. To cope with these psychological stresses women required great confidence and mental resolve. They believed that psychological traits like need for achievement, power, and affiliation were to be developed.

Vibha Sinha (2000) revealed that the number of women longing to take up entrepreneurship had been growing many folds. Most of the women entered this field as first generation women entrepreneurs primarily to remain busy and fulfill their ambition. Women showed to have high single mindedness of purpose to achieve perfection in the quality of their products and services and established their business well.

Vijay Lakhsmi and Poonam Sharma (1980) found that the major problems encumbered by the entrepreneurs were lack of knowledge about the procedure for taking loan and non-implementation of existing policies. The entrepreneurs were highly dissatisfied with the procedure of securing finance and the difficulty factor in acquiring loan was influential contacts, followed by the guarantee cover.

Vinze Dubhashi Medha (1987) studied the socio-economic background and the factors that contributed to entry into business of women entrepreneurs in Delhi. Corroborating with above findings, she highlighted the cultural aspects. It was harder for women to take 'calculated risks' that were essential to entrepreneurship, as they were the custodians of society in the maintenance of cherished values, habits, and accepted norms of conduct.

Vishnuprasad Nagadevara (2009) analyzed the differences between the enterprises owned by women and other enterprises. He used a large database of SSIs and SSSBEs to evaluate the effectiveness and efficiency of the units owned by women and also identified areas where women owned units performed better based on selected performance criteria. Data from more than 1.3 million SSI and SSSBE units were analyzed to identify the differences between women owned enterprises and other enterprises. It was found that the average value of revenue as well as the value of exports was smaller in the enterprises owned by women. In general, there enterprises were smaller in size as compared to other enterprises. On the other hand, the growth of the SSI women enterprises over the past 3 years was significantly higher than that of the other enterprises.

W. Kalyani and K. Chandralekha (2002) attempted to study about women entrepreneurs who took initiatives to start their own enterprises. They also analyzed the factors that motivated women to initiate the launching of enterprises and the factors which supported their effective association in managing the enterprises. The study was based on an exploratory survey on a sample of 300 women entrepreneurs in two urban centres. The result revealed that various socio-economic and demographic characteristics had significant impact on the women entrepreneurs in their enterprise management.

Wesley Carter and Cannon (1992) identified four areas of financing problems for women in their study. Firstly, women were disadvantaged in their ability to raise start-up finance. Secondly, guarantees required for external finance were beyond the scope of most women's personal assets and credit track record. Thirdly, once a business is established, getting finance was more difficult for female entrepreneurs than for their male counterparts, because of the greater difficulties that women faced in penetrating informal financial networks. Finally, the bankers showed discrimination towards women.

Westhead (2003) provided the empirical evidence relating to the wealth contributions of female and male controlled business. His study focused on the performance of business controlled by male or female single decision makers. The total assets and owners' equity was significantly higher for the male-controlled business and also the total income and profit were significantly higher in male-controlled business.

William J. Clinton (1992), in "Lessons without Borders: USAID Shares Micro Enterprise Experience" revealed, "Micro enterprise is a good social policy. It costs the government little or nothing. The enterprises provide income that sustains families and helps finance investment and business growth. They tell us that we need to do a much better job of harnessing the energies of the poor. Not only are their energies a tremendous and underutilized resource, but an approach based on those energies is socially healthy". Furthermore, support for the development of micro enterprises, will be a double positive. It will not only reduce the need for dependence on safety nets but also strengthen the entitlement and capabilities of women.

Zillur Rahman (2005) in his study dealt with the measurement of service quality of banks in India. He investigated the discrepancy between customers' expectations and perceptions towards the quality of services. The study was conducted using the SERVQUAL instrument. The results indicated that the sample population had perpetual problems with their banking service experiences. Findings from this study provided initial direction in determining the optimum service quality attributes to focus on in promoting banking services. The largest discrepancies were found along the reliability dimension. This is alarming, since it was identified as the most important dimension in their overall perceptions.

2.2   Concepts Used

The operational definitions of concepts used in the study are given below:

2.2.1 Entrepreneur

The term 'entrepreneur' is derived from the French word, 'Entrepredre' which means 'to undertake'. The term was first used as a technical economic term by the 18th century French economist Richard Cantillion. He portrayed an entrepreneur as one, discharging the function of direction and speculation. By enlarging the scope, he even quoted "anybody engaged in economic activity was an entrepreneur".

An entrepreneur is a person who has possession of a new enterprise, venture or idea and assumes significant accountability for the inherent risks and the outcome. Entrepreneur in English is a term applied to the type of personality who is willing to take upon him a new venture or enterprise and accepts full responsibility for the outcome. Jean-Baptiste Say, a French economist is believed to have coined the word "entrepreneur" first in about 1800. He said an entrepreneur is "one who undertakes an enterprise, especially a contractor, acting as intermediately between capital and labour".

An entrepreneurial event can be defined as the fact that one or several persons recognize a commercial opportunity in relation to the surroundings, acquire and organize the necessary resources, and coordinate the activities required for exploiting the opportunity commercially. By extension, entrepreneurs may be perceived as the person or persons who initiate and implement the managerial process behind the entrepreneurial event. From a purely statistical point of view, an entrepreneur is defined as a person who establishes a "genuinely new enterprise". This means that the number of entrepreneurs is expressed by the annual influx of personally owned enterprises.

J.B.Say stated, "The entrepreneur is a person endowed with the qualities of judgment, perseverance and knowledge of the world as well as of business". Adam Smith treated the entrepreneur as an employer, master, merchant and undertaker but explicitly identified him with a capitalist.

Brochl G. Wayne stated, "Entrepreneur is an important change agent in every society. Although it is his purposive activity that bridges the gap between plan and reality, the precise way that this change agent (entrepreneur) acts is often unclear".

Peter Dancher defined "... an entrepreneur as one who always searches for change, responds to it and exploits it as an opportunity. Entrepreneurs innovate. Innovation is a specific instrument of entrepreneurship".

Mc. Crony opined that "... a successful entrepreneur lives frugally and saves for the development of his enterprise. He is skilled enough, quality-conscious and very quick to learn from others. He is versatile and resourceful".

According to Mc Clelland, the successful entrepreneurs are endowed with an unusual creativeness, enriched by high property, and a strong need for achievement.

James J. Berna stressed that a good entrepreneur is an enterprising individual. He is energetic, hard working, resourceful, very alert to new opportunities, able enough to adapt to changing conditions with ease and always willing to undertake risks involved in change.

2.2.2 Entrepreneurship

Entrepreneurship is commonly seen as a positive, even pivotal, aspect of economic development. The main argument for the positive effect of entrepreneurship can be found in Schumpeter's work (Schumpeter, 1912) wherein he discusses that by introducing new ideas, products, production processes and organizational structures, entrepreneurs challenge current economic conditions.

Entrepreneurship is the attempt to create value recognitions of business opportunity, the management of risk-taking appropriate to the opportunity and through the communicative and management skills to mobilize human, financial and material resource necessary to bring a project to friction.

Entrepreneurship means the function of seeking investment and production opportunity, organizing an enterprise to undertake a new production process, raising capitals, finding labour, arranging the supply of raw materials, finding site, introducing a new techniques, discovering new sources of raw materials and selecting top managers for day to day operations of the enterprise.

According to William Diamond, "Entrepreneurship is equivalent to enterprise which involves the willingness to assume risks in undertaking an economic activity, particularly a new one. It may involve an innovation, it always involves risk taking, decision making, although neither risk nor decision making may be of great significance.

2.2.3 Women Entrepreneurs

Women entrepreneurs are a woman or a group of women who initiate, organize and operate a business enterprise. The government of India considers the enterprise of women entrepreneurs as "an enterprise owned and controlled by women saving a minimum financial interest of 51 per cent of the capital and giving at least 51 per cent of the employment generated in the enterprise to women".

Women entrepreneurs is defined as an enterprise owned and controlled by one or more women having a minimum financial holding of 51 per cent or more, giving 51 per cent or more employment to women.

Women entrepreneur is any women who organizes and manages any enterprise, especially a business.

Technically, a "women entrepreneur" is any woman who organizes and manages any enterprise, a business, usually with considerable initiative and risk. However, quite often the term "women-owned business" is used relative to government contracting. In this instance, the entrepreneur (a woman) owns (more than 50 per cent), controls and runs the enterprise.

The concept of women entrepreneur enterprise is a small scale industrial unit or industry-related service or business enterprise, managed by one or more women entrepreneurs in a concern, in which they will individually or jointly have a share capital of not less than 51 per cent as shareholders of the private limited company or members of co-operative society".

A small scale industrial unit or Industry related service or business enterprises, managed by one or more women entrepreneurs in proprietary concerns, or in which she/ they individually or jointly have a share capital of not less than 51 per cent as partners or shareholders or directors of private limits company or members of cooperative society.

Women entrepreneur is a person who accepts challenging role to meet her personal needs and become economically independent. A strong desire to do something positive is an inbuilt quality of entrepreneurial women, who is capable of contributing values in both family and social life.

2.2.4 Small Scale Industries

The official definition of an SSI unit in India is a manufacturing enterprise that has investments in fixed assets in plant and machinery of less than INR 10 million (US$ 222,000).

Small Scale Industries is an industrial undertaking in which the investment in fixed assets in plant and machinery whether held on ownership terms on lease or on hire purchase does not exceed Rs10 million.

The definition for small scale industries has changed over time. Initially they were classified into two categories - those using power with less than 50 employees and those not using power with the employee strength being more than 50 but less than 100. However the capital resources invested on plant and machinery buildings have been the primary criteria to differentiate the small scale industries from the large and medium scale industries. An industrial unit can be categorized as a small scale unit if it fulfils the capital investment limit fixed by the government of India for the small scale sector. As per the latest definition, for any industrial unit to be regarded as small scale industrial unit the following condition is to be satisfied: "Investment in fixed assets like plants and equipments either held on ownership terms on lease or on hire purchase should not be more than Rs10 million. However the unit in no way can be owned or controlled by any other industrial unit.

Small scale industry means an industry that employs capital less than Rs1 crore. Almost all items can be manufactured in a small scale industry, but there are large scale manufacturing activities like rolling mills, extrusion presses, pilger mills etc., that cost much more.

The European Union definition of a small scale enterprise is one with fewer than 50 employees and less than 10 million euros in annual turnover or balance sheet total.

A small scale industry is defined as an industrial undertaking in which the investment in fixed assets in plant and machinery, whether held on ownership terms or on lease or on hire purchase, does not exceed RsOne Crore.

Small scale industry is defined as an industrial undertaking which is engaged or is proposed to be engaged in the manufacturing or production of parts, components, sub-assemblies, tooling or intermediates, or the rendering of services, and undertaking supplies or proposes to supply or renders not more than 50 per cent of its production or services, as the case may be, to one or more industrial undertakings and whose investment in fixed assets in plant and machinery, whether held on ownership terms or on lease or on hire purchase, does not exceed Rs one Crore.

Small scale service and business enterprises are defined as industry related service and business enterprises with investment in fixed assets, excluding land and building up to Rs5 lakhs.

2.3 Summary

A review of the past research studies and literature available relating to the study and the operational definitions of the concepts used are presented in this chapter. The review facilitated the researcher to have a comprehensive knowledge on the subject taken for the study. The operational definitions of the concepts used helped the researcher as steering to perform the study in the correct direction. On line journals in the field of women entrepreneurship, small business management, marketing research, economic development, socio-economic and applied psychology were referred to enrich the knowledge.

The above mentioned studies are related to the socio-economic conditions of women entrepreneurs and their problems like finance, marketing, work-family conflicts, push and pull factors, profitability of the enterprise, comparison of men and women entrepreneurs and the like. Moreover, all these studies are descriptive in nature. However, there are no comprehensive and analytical studies covering the developmental factors of women entrepreneurs, in different angles in Tirunelveli district in Tamil Nadu. Hence, the researcher has made an attempt to explore the developmental factors of women entrepreneurs, by applying relevant statistical tools, to test the development attributes. The empirical study also covers the constraints of women entrepreneurs and perception of women entrepreneurs on bank services in the study area. Therefore, this study is first of its kind in the field of women entrepreneurs in Tirunelveli district in Tamil Nadu.

CHAPTER III

PROFILE OF THE STUDY AREA AND SMALL

SCALE INDUSTRIES

This chapter deals with the profile of the study area such as history, physical features, geographical location of the district, administrative arrangement in the district, demographic characteristics, land utilization, transport services, educational services, industries and trade, commerce and export in the area. It is very essential and important to know about the background and the plight of the study area on various aspects to understand the problem better, frame the interview schedules and cognizance of the findings of the research and its 'cause and effect' relationship.

3.1   Tirunelveli District

Tirunelveli, the penultimate southern most district of Tamil Nadu, is described as a microcosm of the state, owing to its mosaic and diverse geographical and physical features such as lofty mountains and low plains, dry Teri structures, rivers and cascades, seacoast and thick inland forest, sandy soils and fertile alluvium, a variety of flora, fauna, and protected wild life.

History

The history of this district is bound up with that of the Pandya just like Madurai and Ramanathapuram areas. Even earlier, a pre-historic race is said to have occupied this land. During the later half of the 18th century, the East India Company was frequently at war with the Poligars on behalf of the Carnatic Nawab in Tirunelveli and Madurai. With the fall of Tippu in 1799, British concentrated their force in the south and suppressed the Poligars. At about this time, the Nawab of Carnatic became powerless and left the management of the territory to the British. The Nawab was pensioned off and the management of the revenues of Tirunelveli was made over to the British in 1801 under a treaty. Thus the British rule started which lasted till 1947. Before the establishment of British rule, the Portuguese and Dutch occupied Thoothukudi and other port areas. After the British rule, Swaraj movement was started and a number of prominent persons of this district fought against the British and clamoured for independence of the country. In the year 1986 the district was divided into two parts namely Tirunelveli and Thoothukudi vide State Government Notification G.O. Ms.No.1314 dated 27-9-86. Main languages spoken in the district are Tamil and Telugu.

Geography and Physical Features

The prominent hills are part of the Western Ghats and form the boundary between Kerala State and this district on the western side. The Western Ghats run to a length of about 160 km. in the district starting from the north-western part in Sankarankoil Taluk and ending at about 15 km. from Kanyakumari. Valuable trees are found in the Western Ghats. The Western Ghats lie on the western part of Sankarankoil, Tenkasi and Ambasamudram taluks. Near the border of Tenkasi and Ambasamudram taluks, the ghats widen forming undulating hills, broad valleys and extensive plateau. The height of the hills diminishes considerably near Shencottai and permits communication by road and rail to places in Kerala through the Shencottai pass. Besides this, a portion of the range lies on the southern part of Ambasamudram taluk and in the western and southern portions of Nanguneri taluk, it diminishes in height at Aramboly permitting road communication with Kanyakumari. The hills of the Western Ghats have valuable trees, which are being exploited for commercial purposes. The conspicuous among the hills are Kallakadai Mottai (5721feet) above Sivagiri, Kottaimalai (6335 feet) over Puliyangudi and Kuliratti (5876 feet) near Kadayanallur Krishnapuram. Thamiraparani river rises in the Agasthiyamalai (Pothigai hills) of the Western Ghats and descends to the plains at Papanasam in Ambasamudram taluk. The height of the Agasthiamalai is 6132 feet and is considered as the seat of the Saint Agasthiyar who was said to be conducting research in Tamil language.

Geographical Location of the District

Tirunelveli district is bounded by Virudhunagar district in the North, Kerala State and Kanyakumari district in the West, Gulf of Mannar in the South and Tuticorin district in the East. The district lies between 80 10' and 90 40' north latitude and 770 21' and 770 99' east longitude. The general geographical formation of the district is hill area. Thamiraparani River and Chittar River are flowing in the district. Thamiraparani River is a perennial river whereas Chittar River will be dry during the summer season.

The total geographical area of the district is about 681657 sq.km. The district is divided into 19 blocks. The name of the taluks and area are shown in the Table 3.1.

Table 3.1

Name & Area of the Taluks and Area in Tirunelveli District

S.No.	Name of Taluks	Area in Sq. Km.
1	Ambasamudram	1910.60
2	Shencottai	162.54
3	Sivagiri	371.62
4	Sankarankoil	714.81
5	Radhapuram	642.55
6	Tirunelveli	264.79
7	Nanguneri	1311.74
8	Palayamkotti	440.94
9	Tenkasi	996.98
	District Total Area	**6816.57**

Source: District Profile during 2009 – 10

Administrative Arrangement in the District

The Tirunelveli district comprises of 9 taluks, 19 blocks and 1717 villages. As regards the hierarchy of administrative arrangement, there are 1 corporation, 6 municipalities, 37 Town Panchayats and 424 village panchayats in the district. The community development blocks are Vasudevanallur, Sankarankovil, Kuruvikulam, Melaneelithanallur, Shencottai, Tenkasi, Alangulam, Keelapavoor, Kadaiyanallur, Manur, Palayamkottai, Ambasamudram, Kadayam, Pappakudi, Cherenmahadevi, Nanguneri, Kalakadu, Radhapuram and Valliyoor.

Demographic Characteristics of the District

The population of Tirunelveli district grew from 16,98,578 in 1961 to 27,40,065 in 1991. The growth rate indicates that there has been a significant increase during the 1981-91 decade with the average growth rate being 2.33% per annum during this decade. According to the 1991 census Tenkasi taluk is the most populated and Shencottai taluk is the least populated in the district. The area and the population in the

19 blocks of the district are summarized in the table 3.2 overleaf according to the 2001 census of the Government of India. The table 3.3 summarized the Number of literates in the District.

Table 3.2

Features of Area and Population of Tirunelveli District – Block Wise Details

S.No	Name of the Block	Area (Sq.km)	Population		
			Total	Male	Female
1	Manur	493.43	508364	250022	258342
2	Palayamkottai	371.62	98185	48757	49428
3	Sankarankoil	293.54	146648	72671	73977
4	Melaneelithanallur	317.83	87168	42943	44225
5	Kuruvikulam	468.44	106995	52607	54388
6	Tenkasi	216.60	171638	85134	86504
7	Alangulam	324.65	116981	56815	60166
8	Keelepavur	207.76	161631	80091	81540
9	Vasudevanallr	568.90	177852	87559	90293
10	Shencottai	189.22	101957	50989	50968
11	Ambasamuthram	734.84	14287	69871	72316
12	Cheranmahadevi	197.93	123848	60369	63479
13	Pappakudi	162.54	71124	34479	36645
14	Kadayanallur	264.79	140933	69333	71600
15	Kadayam	195.40	97728	47362	50356
16	Nanguneri	502.59	106767	51268	55499
17	Kalakadu	440.94	197614	46717	50897
18	Valliyoor	425.92	148019	70970	77049
19	Radhapuram	474.76	116576	55090	61486
	TOTAL	**6823.08**	**2723988**	**1333939**	**1390049**

Source: District Profile during 2009 – 10 (2001 CENSUS)

Table 3.3

Number of Literates in the District – Block Wise Details

S.No	Name of the Block	Literate		
		Total	Male	Female
1	Manur	373203	198736	174467
2	Palayamkottai	50203	27550	22653
3	Sankarankoil	94127	42255	51876
4	Melaneelithanallur	47909	27924	19985
5	Kuruvikulam	63653	36954	26699
6	Tenkasi	117098	65046	52052
7	Alangulam	70511	39654	30857
8	Keelepavur	103251	58207	43044
9	Vasudevanallr	103783	60494	43289
10	Shencottai	65783	37431	28352
11	Ambasamuthram	106144	56632	49512
12	Cheranmahadevi	88689	47313	41376
13	Pappakudi	46653	25257	21402
14	Kadayanallur	85069	49114	35955
15	Kadayam	64174	35113	29061
16	Naguneri	77199	39344	37865
17	Kalakadu	32417	16955	15462
18	Valliyoor	106507	54170	52337
19	Radhapuram	83506	41104	42402
	TOTAL	**1829064**	**997278**	**831786**

Source: District Profile during 2009 – 10 (2001 CENSUS)

Land Utilization:

Paddy is cultivated mainly in Sankarankoil, Tirunelveli, Tenkasi, Shencottai, Ambasamudram and Nanguneri taluks. Maize, millet and Kudiraivali are being cultivated in the dry tracts of this district namely Sivagiri and part of Sankarankoil taluks. Cotton is being cultivated mainly in Sankarankoil taluk. Cropped area accounts for about 20.91 per cent of the total area. Forestlands cover about 17.62 per cent of the total land. A significant portion (48.06 per cent) of the land falls under the category of 'non available for cultivation' and 'fallow lands'.

Transport Services

Transport services play a vital role in the economic development of the nation opening up remote areas, stimulating the growth of agriculture as well as industry, besides facilitating communication. Transport services also contribute to the growth of the nation's economy.

The road network in Tirunelveli district consists of national highways (94.000 km), national highways (A1) (181.00 km), state highways (561.039 km), corporation and municipalities road (1001.54 km), panchayat union and panchayat road (1658.35 km), town panchayat and townships road (863.51 km) and forest roads (114.450 km). The national highway road from Madras to Nagercoil connects the district headquarter with Madurai, Virudhunader and Nagercoil and also connects the main cities within the Tirunelveli district. The railway network in Tirunelveli district consists of broad gauge (95.448 km) and metre gauge (134.430 km). Tirunelveli district consists of totally 27 railway stations.

Educational Services

Tirunelveli district, or more specifically, Palayamkottai, is called the Oxford of South India as the city has excellent educational institutions. The Manonmaniam Sundaranar University is named after the famous poet who penned the Tamil Thai Vazhthu, the official song of the state. This University has 26 departments, and offers some unique courses in Tamil Nadu, like Criminology and Criminal justice.

In view of improving the quality of technical education in the southern parts of Tamil Nadu, Anna University Tirunelveli was established in 2007. The University offers a variety of engineering and technology courses in both undergraduate and postgraduate streams. Research facilities are being established in a start-of-the-art campus near Palayamkottai. The district has many prestigious old government and private colleges in the medical, legal, engineering, arts, pharmaceutical and physiotherapy fields. School education is by the government and private managements in the district.

Table 3.4

Number of Educational Institutions in the District

S.No	Educational Institutions	Total Number
1	Universities	2
2	Arts and Science Colleges	25
3	Medical Colleges	2
4	Physiotherapy College	1
5	Engineering Colleges	12
6	Law College	1
7	Pre Kindergarten Schools	201
8	Primary Schools	1521
9	Middle Schools	394
10	High Schools	114
11	Higher Secondary Schools	150
12	Teacher Training Institutes	26

Source: District Profile during 2009 – 10

Industries

Though the main occupation of the people is cultivation, in recent years industries and services are also competing with this ancient occupation. M/s. India Cements of Thalaiyuthu, Co-operative Spinning Mills situated at Pettai and other spinning mills in Ambasamudram and Thoothukudi, Sun Paper Mill of Cheranmahadevi, Dharani Sugar mill at Vasudevanallur are a few large scale industrial units functioning in the district. The industries prevalent in the district may be classified under (i) household industries (ii) small scale and (iii) medium and large-scale industries. Beedi rolling, safety matches making, mat weaving and processing and manufacture of palm fiber and articles from palm trees and handloom weaving of textiles are the main household industries. Workers in household industries are concentrated mostly in Tenkasi, Ambasamudram and Tirunelveli taluks. Safety matches are manufactured mainly in Sankarankoil and Sivagiri taluks. Handloom weaving is prominent in Ambasamudram and Tenkasi taluk. Beedi rolling and mat weaving are chiefly found in Tenkasi, Ambasamudram and Tirunelveli taluks. Manufacturing of articles from palm trees is mainly found in Nanguneri taluk where palmyrah trees cover large areas.

Trade, Commerce and Export

Even before independence the people of this district were very much interested in trade and commerce. History says that pearls and chanks available in coastal parts were sent abroad through Thuthukudi. Chilly, groundnut, cotton and safety matches from the northern parts of the district and fruits, beedi, mats, handloom clothes, toys and yarn from central areas are transported to other parts of the State for sale. Cattle are exported to Kerala from the district. Tirunelveli and Sankarankoil are the main business centres of the district. Toys of Ambasamudram and palm leaf products of the coastal parts of this district are fine hand works which are liked by the foreigners and are also items much in demand. The palm Jaggery, palm leaf products, some varieties of mats, fish and lungies are also exported to foreign countries. Cement produced at the India Cements Company is sent to other districts of the State. The Bank of Tamil Nadu which originated in this district is the leading bank to serve trade and commerce. In addition, some co-operative banks are also helping to improve the trade. M/s. Pandian Grama Bank, a unit of Indian Overseas Bank has taken much effort to improve the district's trade and commerce. There are many commercial banks in the district.

3.2   Small Scale Industries in Tamil Nadu

Tamil Nadu is one among the few states that adopted the strategy of industrial growth with emphasis on small scale industries. The average annual growth in number of units is 12.8 per cent and employment generation around 10.6 per cent. The state has always laid stress on the harmonious development of both large and small industries to reduce disparities in sectoral stabilization and uniform economic development. As employment in the agricultural sector is stagnant and large industry sector is passing through 'zero employment growth', the Government's policy is focused towards the promotion of Agro-based and Food Processing Industry which has a three pronged advantages, namely, promotion of SSI in rural areas by utilizing local resources, creation of rural employment and uplift of rural economy by way of value addition to the area specific produce.

The SSI sector covers a wide range of enterprises with diverse characteristics. There are tiny and micro enterprises on the one hand and sophisticated modern small scale units on the other. A good part of the SSI units get registered under Factories Act and hence gets covered under Annual Survey of Industries (ASI). The units in this SSI Sector are also registered with the State Level Directorates of Industries and Commerce and data for this category get collected from time to time on a census or sample basis. As on 31.3.05, there are 4.89 lakh registered SSI units in Tamilnadu having an investment of Rs14,397 crores, providing employment to 35.25 lakh persons. The Tamil Nadu government has developed various departments and boards to promote and manage the small scale industries in the state. The table 3.5 summarized the small scale industries (Registered) in Tamil Nadu as on 31.03.2010.

Table 3.5

Small Scale Industries (Registered) in Tamil Nadu as on 31.03.2010

Details of Industrial Classification	No. of Units	Value (Rs. in Lakhs)		Employment In Number
		Investment	Production	
Food Products	45070	95831	1147126	219007
Beverages and Tobacco Products	3037	5145	155705	80242
Cotton Textiles	28527	77980	854881	209378
Wool, Silk, Synthetic, Fiber Textiles	2966	14384	223490	47025
Jute, Hemp, Mesta Products	1775	64590	145913	58414
Hosiery and Readymade Garments	143074	271377	2726443	1182967
Wood and Wood Products	22216	44029	279078	106543
Paper and Paper Products	30089	90569	456657	127926

Leather Industries	13332	54058	438044	162225
Rubber and Plastic Products	17062	51671	37042	95941
Chemical and Chemical Products	20781	43358	362475	276109
Non-metallic Mineral Products	14732	36282	203205	158978
Basic Mineral Products	6993	32238	180028	67696
Metal Products and Parts	26832	75794	450356	186800
Machinery & Parts except Electrical	32858	74306	487995	132888
Electrical Machinery Apparatus	14069	73377	343093	114239
Transport Equipment and Parts	13261	49592	215293	112523
Other Manufacturing Industries	93878	527111	1891127	364507

Source: Industries Commissioner and Director of Industries and Commerce, Chennai-5. Retrieved from www.tanstia.org.in/download_notifications.pdf

Micro, Small and Medium Enterprises Board

The Small Scale Industries board functioning under the chairmanship of Hon'ble Minister for Rural Industries hitherto has been re-designated as Micro, Small and Medium Enterprises Board based on G.O. (D) No.81, MSME Department dated 11.9.2008. The new MSME Board functions under the chairmanship of Hon'ble Minister for Rural Industries and Animal Husbandry with the chief secretary to government as Vice Chairman. It takes measures to redress the grievances of the MSM enterprises and for their development in the competitive environment. The board includes 17 high level officials of various departments as official members, and 12 MSME and SSI associations as non-official members and 6 high level officials of state and central government organizations serve as members of the MSME board. The industries commissioner and director of industries and commerce is the member secretary and the official convener of the board. This board meets once in six months to analyze the problems and issues of MSMEs rose by the MSME associations and suggest suitable solution and then send its recommendations to the government. The last MSME board meeting was held on 9.3.2009 under the chairmanship of Honorable Minister for Rural Industries and Animal Husbandry.

Tamil Nadu Small Industries Development Corporation Ltd. (TANSIDCO)

The government of Tamil Nadu established Tamil Nadu Small Industries Development Corporation Limited (TANSIDCO) in 1970 in order to assist micro, small and medium enterprises and to protect and promote the interests of micro, small and medium enterprises in the state.

Prior to the establishment of TANSIDCO, 35 industrial estates were established by the government of Tamilnadu through Directorate of Industries and Commerce. On formation of TANSIDCO, these 35 industrial estates were transferred to TANSIDCO on agency terms during 1974 as per G.O. Ms. No.720 Industries (Spl) dated 17.5.1974. Also TANSIDCO has established 43 industrial estates on its own and thus there are 78 industrial estates under the control of TANSIDCO. Apart from these 78 industrial estates, to create more opportunity for the development of micro, small and medium enterprises in all the districts in Tamilnadu, 22 new industrial estates were proposed. Out of these 22 new industrial estates, works were taken up in 14 industrial estates and for the remaining 8 industrial estates land acquisition and alienation works are in progress. TANSIDCO identifies places and districts where there is possibility of industrial growth and takes action to form industrial estates and thereby it guides the micro small enterprises entrepreneurs in the promotion of industries.

At present, 92 industrial estates are being administered by Tamil Nadu Small Industries Development Corporation throughout Tamil Nadu. These industrial estates spread over an area of 6947.37 acres. There are 6658 developed plots and 4385 sheds in all these industrial estates. Totally, 2,24,181 employees have got employment in these industrial estates, the male employees being 1,01,906 and female employees being 1,22,275. The annual turn over of the units functioning in these industrial estates is Rs11,433 crores, out of which the value of the goods being exported is Rs3,112 crores. They have generated an income of Rs1,080 crores to the state government and Rs660 crores to the central government.

Directorate of Industries and Commerce

The Directorate of Industries and Commerce is the nodal government agency responsible for planning and implementation of various programmes for small scale and tiny industries. In the past, the role of the Directorate was most statutory and regulatory in nature, sanctioning license, and issue of raw materials during time of scarcity. It has acquired a development orientation now. Most of the operational powers have been delegated to the General Managers of the District Industries Centre and time limits have been prescribed for various Government clearances necessary to an industry.

District Industries Centre

Out of 32 revenue districts, District Industries Centres (DIC) are functioning in 30 districts in Tamil Nadu, except Chennai District where a Regional Joint Directorate is set up to render all help to the entrepreneurs to set up small scale industries. DICs administer the various incentive programmes such as capital subsidies, fiscal incentives, raw material allocations, power subsidies and the like. The DICs are expected to function as key conduits for information flowing from various channels for dissemination to local enterprises. To facilitate smooth establishment of small scale units and to reduce procedural wrangles, the government has launched single window scheme. The entrepreneurs are assisted in getting clearances from local bodies, town planning, pollution control board, public health, factories and other departments and getting power connection by the single window authority.

3.3   Small Scale Industries in Tirunelveli District

There are about 2300 small scale industries in Tirunelveli District. Of all the 18 major groups, units manufacturing chemical products alone account for nearly one third. Next comes the manufacture of food products and under food products salt industry forms about one third of the total number of registered units. The chief items produced by large scale industries in the district are cement, cotton yarn, textiles, chemicals and chemical products. M/s. India Cements Limited has two plants, one in Sankarnagar and another in Thalaiyuthu for producing cement. The production of "Portland Cement" in 1979 was more than 13 lakh of tonnes. There are more than 20 textile mills situated in this district for the production of yarn. The first spinning mill under co-operative moment was established in this district during 1958 at Pettai. Most of them are situated in Ambasamudram, Tirunelveli, and Nanguneri taluks. Tamil Nadu Sugar Corporation Limited has established a factory at Tirunelveli, which has a capacity to crush 1250 tonnes of cane a day.

Table 3.6

Registered Entrepreneurs in Tirunelveli District

S.No	Name of the Block	Details of Enterprises in each Block			
		Registered Units	Land & Building (Rs in Lakhs)	Plant & Machinery (Rs in Lakhs)	Employment Generated
1	Ambasamudram	1010	631.49	490.00	5599
2	Alangulam	533	407.00	330.00	1880
3	Cheranmadevi	311	243.80	200.00	1410
4	Kalakad	302	242.90	300	1195
5	Kuruvikulam	699	196.00	520.00	4260
6	Keelapavoor	848	206.18	987.00	3740
7	Kadayam	332	466.55	160.00	1860
8	Kadayanallur	541	244.00	390	2275
9	Meelaneelitha Nallur	319	1694.77	210.00	1485
10	Manur	2080	228.00	2220.00	8551
11	Nanguneri	475	220.00	313.00	1745
12	Pappakudi	363	3220.00	200.00	2485
13	Palayamkottai	3114	764.00	1268.00	17409
14	Radhapuram	573	446.83	590	2126
15	Shencottai	1160	909.05	720.00	6416
16	Sankarankovil	1207	1712.48	823.00	6550
17	Tenkasi	986	1050.24	880.00	4126
18	Vasudevanallur	943	594.34	410.00	2899
19	Valliyoor	876	926.00	1430.00	2555
	TOTAL	**16672**	**14403.63**	**12441**	**78566**

Source: District Industries Centre (DIC), Tirunelveli as on 31.07.2008

District Industries Centre (DIC), Tirunelveli

The Tirunelveli District Industries Centre was formed to gear up industrialization and render all assistance required for the setting up of new units under one roof in the district. The District Industries Centre has been functioning in this district from 1st July 1978. It provides assistance to small-scale industries in the sphere of finance, getting clearance for various licenses, registration, incentives and loan assistance offered by the Government of Tamil Nadu. The District Industries Centre assists entrepreneurs in selecting viable industries, provides project reports, registers provisional small scale industrial units, permanent units and ancillary units and gets clearance for various licenses through a single window clearance committee. It provides information to entrepreneurs relating to machinery, buyer and seller details facilitates hire purchase of machinery with assistance from the National Small Scale Industries Corporation and helps in the import of capital goods, machinery spares and raw materials. It makes arrangement for finance through banks and other financial institutions, and arranges seed money assistance from financial institutions. Through Entrepreneur Development Training Programme, it guides the entrepreneurs in starting new industries and provides technical information and guidance. It provides margin money assistance to sick units under the Sick Industries Rehabilitation Programme. It conducts motivation campaign in panchayat union areas and identifies entrepreneurs.

3.4 Summary

The profile of the study area and the development and organization of the Small Scale Industries in Tamil Nadu and particularly in Tirunelveli district are presented in this chapter. The historical background, the origin, the administrative set up, demographic characteristics, educational potential, and industries, trade, commerce and export of the district are explained in the chapter.

CHAPTER IV

ANALYSIS AND INTERPRETATION OF PERSONAL PROFILE AND ORGANIZATIONAL PROFILE

This chapter deals with the analysis and interpretations of personal profile and organizational profile of the enterprises of the respondents in Tirunelveli district. The descriptive analysis of the personal profile is done in the first part and the organizational profile of the enterprise is done in the final part of the chapter. Percentage analysis has been used to analyze the profile and the background of women entrepreneurs, the organizational profile of enterprise and to draw inferences. In the percentage analysis, based on the woman entrepreneur's role in the management of the enterprise the sample units are divided into three categories: (1) Women Managed Units (WMU), (2) Jointly Managed Units (JMU) and (3) Men Managed Units (MMU) for the purpose of the analyses.

In a developing country like India, a favorable socio-economic environment could help in exploiting the latent entrepreneurial talents. However, the unfavourable conditions often hinder the emergence of such entrepreneurial talents. Despite these situational constraints, today many people enter the field of entrepreneurship in India. The entrepreneurial behaviour and enterprise management among the people are supported and sustained by the growth of enterprise involvement by the demographic and environmental factors among the respondents. Such information is expected to provide for a mechanism to identify the people who have the potential and plan appropriate training programmes to develop their potential further.

Aida Idris (2008) framed the object for his research and generated a profile of innovative Malaysian women entrepreneurs based on certain personal factors such as age, level of education, and marital status.

Shiva Malik and Taranjit Kaur Rao (2008) analyzed the socio-economic profile of women entrepreneurs of Chandigarh based their age, education level, marital status and nature of family. Hence, the present part of the study focuses on the profile of the respondents.

4.1 DESCRIPTIVE ANALYSIS OF PERSONAL PROFILE

4.1.1 Types of Ownership of the Respondents

The respondents are classified into three types based on the ownership of the enterprises units: 1) Women Managed Unit (WMU) which strictly comes under the description of a Woman enterprise under WIP (Women Industries Programme). These units are owned and managed by women and give at least 80 per cent of the employment generated in the enterprise to women. 2) Jointly Managed Unit (JMU) in which women have 50 per cent say in all aspects of management and at least 50 per cent of the employment generated in the enterprise goes to women. 3) Men Managed Unit (MMU) is women's enterprise only in name. They are *dejure* 'entrepreneurs' who not even know much about the enterprise and play a little or no role in management irrespective of whether the employees are women or not. Based on the reviews, three variables are created with respect to the type of ownership. The respondents were asked to tick the appropriate variables after brief explanation of the meaning of each variable. The distribution of the respondents on the basis of their ownership is shown in table 4.1.

Table 4.1

Types of Ownership of the Respondents

S.No	Types of Ownership	Number of Respondents	Percentage
1.	Women Managed Units (WMU)	238	62.63
2.	Jointly Managed Units (JMU)	104	27.37
3.	Men Managed Units (MMU)	38	10
Total		**380**	**100**

Source: Primary data

The above table reveals that 62.63 per cent of the respondents are in the ownership group of Women Managed Units (WMU) followed by 27.37 per cent in the ownership group of Jointly Managed Units (JMU) and 10 per cent in the ownership group of Men Managed Units (MMU). The analysis infers that the dominant ownership group among the respondents is Women Managed Units (WMU).

4.1.2 Age of the Respondents

Age is the accumulation of changes in an organism or object over time. Age in humans refers to a multidimensional process of physical, psychological, and social change. Some dimensions of age grow and expand over time, while others decline. Age is an important part of all human societies reflecting the biological changes that occur, but also reflecting cultural and societal conventions. In this way these aspects influence the development of entrepreneur also. Since the age of the respondents influences the entrepreneurship, it is included in the present study. The age of the respondents is classified as 25 years and below, 26 – 35 years, 36 – 45 years, 46 – 55 years, and above 55 years. The distribution of the respondents on the basis of their age is shown in table 4.2.

Table 4.2

Age of the Respondents

S.No	Age (In Years)	Number of Respondents			Total
		WMU	JMU	MMU	
1.	25 and below	24 (10.08)	8 (7.69)	4 (10.53)	36 (9.47)
2.	26 – 35	42 (17.65)	37 (35.58)	7 (18.42)	86 (22.63)
3.	36 – 45	74 (31.09)	15 (14.42)	12 (31.58)	101 (26.58)
4.	46 – 55	60 (25.21)	32 (30.77)	6 (15.79)	98 (25.79)
5.	Above 55	38 (15.97)	12 (11.54)	9 (23.68)	59 (15.53)
	Total	**238**	**104**	**38**	**380**

Source: Primary data

Table 4.2 shows the age distribution of the respondents. The above table reveals that the dominant age groups among the respondents are 36 – 45 and 46 – 55 which constitute 26.58 and 25.79 per cent respectively followed by the age group of 26 – 35, above 55 and 25 and below which constitute 22.63, 15.53 and 9.47 per cent respectively. The age group of 25 and below is very small.

Among the women managed units, the dominant age groups are 36 – 45 and 46 – 55 which constitute 31.09 and 25.21 per cent respectively followed by the age group of 26 – 35, above 55 and 25 and below which constitute 17.65, 15.97 and 10.08 per cent respectively. Among the jointly managed units, the dominant age groups are 26 – 35 and 46 – 55 which constitute 35.58 and 30.77 per cent respectively followed by the age group of 36 – 45, above 55 and 25 and below which constitute 14.42, 11.54 and 7.69 per cent respectively. Among the men managed units, the dominant age groups are 36 – 45 and above 55 which constitute 31.58 and 23.68 per cent respectively, followed by the age group of 26 – 35, 46 – 55 and 25 and below which constitute 18.42, 15.79 and 10.53 per cent respectively.

4.1.3   Educational Level of the Respondents

Education makes an entrepreneur a right thinker and a correct decision-maker in his enterprise. Since the level of education is one of the determining factors for the development of women entrepreneurs, it is included in the present study. The level of education of the respondents is grouped as SSLC, higher secondary level, under graduate level, post graduate level and technical level. The distribution of the respondents on the basis of their education level is shown in table 4.3.

Table 4.3

Educational Level of the Respondents

S.No	Educational Level	Number of Respondents			Total
		WMU	JMU	MMU	
1.	SSLC	19 (7.98)	12 (11.54)	6 (15.79)	37 (9.74)
2.	Higher Secondary Level	26 (10.92)	24 (23.08)	7 (18.42)	57 (15)
3.	Under Graduate Level	95 (39.92)	32 (30.16)	10 (26.32)	137 (36.05)
4.	Post Graduate Level	58 (24.37)	17 (16.35)	7 (18.42)	82 (21.58)
5.	Technical Level	40 (16.81)	19 (18.27)	8 (21.05)	67 (17.63)
	Total	238	104	38	380

Source: Primary data

It is found from the above table that the majority of the respondents in the study area (36.05 per cent) come under graduate level. The second important category is the group of respondents who completed post graduate level which constitutes 21.58 per cent followed by the technical level, higher secondary level and SSLC level groups which constitute 17.63, 15 and 9.74 per cent respectively.

Among the women managed units, under graduate level and post graduate level are the dominant education groups which constitute 39.92 and 24.37 per cent respectively, followed by the technical level, higher secondary level and SSLC level groups which constitute 16.81, 10.92 and 7.98 per cent respectively. Among the jointly managed units, under graduate level and higher secondary level are the dominant education groups which constitute 30.16 and 23.08 per cent respectively, followed by the technical level, post graduate level and SSLC level groups which constitute 18.27, 16.35 and 11.54 per cent respectively. Among the men managed units, under graduate level and technical level are the dominant education groups which constitute 26.32 and

21.05 per cent respectively, followed by the post graduate level, higher secondary level and SSLC level groups which constitute 18.42, 18.42 and 15.79 per cent respectively.

4.1.4 Marital Status of the Respondents

Marital status of the respondents may influence the need of money, inspiration, perception, personality factors, mode of earning and determination in their enterprises. According to the marital status of the respondents, the psychological and physiological framework may change. Since these aspects influence the development of the respondents, it is included in the study. Marital status of the respondents is classified into unmarried, recently married, married, widow and separated. Recently married is considered the respondents who got the marriage within one year while interviewing. The distribution of the respondents on the basis of their marital status is shown in table 4.4

Table 4.4

Marital Status of the Respondents

S.No	Marital Status	Number of Respondents			Total
		WMU	JMU	MMU	
1.	Unmarried	32 (13.45)	18 (17.31)	6 (15.79)	56 (14.74)
2.	Recently Married	25 (10.5)	12 (11.54)	13 (34.21)	50 (13.16)
3.	Married	157 (65.97)	41 (39.42)	16 (42.11)	214 (56.31)
4.	Widow	16 (6.72)	20 (19.23)	3 (7.89)	39 (10.26)
5.	Separated	8 (3.36)	13 (12.5)	0 (0)	21 (5.53)
	Total	**238**	**104**	**38**	**380**

Source: Primary data

Table 4.4 shows the marital status of the respondents. More than half of the respondents (56.31 per cent) are married. It is also inferred from the above table that the 14.74 per cent of the respondents is unmarried followed, by the recently married, widow and separated groups which constitute 13.16, 10.26 and 5.53 per cent respectively.

Among the women managed units, married and unmarried are the dominant groups which constitute 65.97 and 13.45 per cent respectively, followed by the recently married, widow and separated groups which constitute 10.5, 6.72 and 3.36 per cent respectively. Among the jointly managed units, married and widow are the dominant groups which constitute 39.42 and 19.23 per cent respectively, followed by the unmarried, separated and recently married groups which constitute 17.31, 12.5 and 11.54 per cent respectively. Among the men managed units, married and recently married are the dominant groups which constitute 42.11 and 34.21 per cent respectively, followed by the unmarried, widow and separated groups which constitute 15.79, 7.89 and 0 per cent respectively.

4.1.5 Nature of the Family

Nature of the family is also one of the factors which affect the magnitude of the development of the respondents. It is classified as nuclear and joint families. Depends upon the classification both have their merits and demerits in development of the enterprise. The respondents from nuclear families have to stand on their own legs whereas the respondents from joint families get support from their family members. Based on these aspects, it is included in the study. The distribution of the respondents on the basis of their nature of the family is shown in table 4.5.

Table 4.5

Nature of the Family

S.No	Nature of the Family	Number of Respondents			Total
		WMU	**JMU**	**MMU**	
1.	Nuclear	181 (76.05)	85 (81.73)	29 (76.32)	295 (77.63)
2.	Joint	57 (23.95)	19 (18.27)	9 (23.68)	85 (22.37)
	Total	**238**	**104**	**38**	**380**

Source: Primary data

The above table shows that 77.63 per cent of the respondents belong to the nuclear family system and 22.37 per cent belong to the joint family system. Among the women managed units, 76.05 per cent are nuclear family system and 23.95 per cent are joint family system. Among the jointly managed units, 81.73 per cent are nuclear family system and 18.27 per cent are joint family system. Among the men managed units, 76.32 per cent are nuclear family system and 23.68 per cent are joint family system.

4.1.6 Size of the Family

The size of the family represents the number of family members living with the respondents under the same roof. It is a vital factor which influences directly the development of women entrepreneurs in their enterprises. Depending upon the size of the family of the respondents, the expenses, expectations, needs, finances, social commitments and infrastructure undergo a tremendous change in their routine life. Since the size of the family is directly associated with the development of the women entrepreneurs, it is included in the study. The size of the family is classified into five groups, namely below 3, 3 – 4, 5 – 6, 7 – 8 and above 8. The distribution of the respondents on the basis of their size of the family is shown in table 4.6.

Table 4.6

Size of the Family

S.No	Size of the Family	Number of Respondents			Total
		WMU	JMU	MMU	
1.	Below 3	41 (17.23)	22 (21.15)	4 (10.53)	67 (17.63)
2.	3 – 4	98 (41.18)	46 (44.23)	18 (47.37)	162 (42.63)
3.	5 – 6	49 (20.59)	18 (17.31)	8 (21.05)	75 (19.74)
4.	7 – 8	31 (13.02)	12 (11.54)	5 (13.16)	48 (12.63)
5.	Above 8	19 (7.98)	6 (5.77)	3 (7.89)	28 (7.37)
	Total	**238**	**104**	**38**	**380**

Source: Primary data

It is understood from the above table that the dominant groups among the respondents are 3 – 4 and 5 – 6 which constitute 42.63 and 19.74 per cent respectively, followed by the below 3, 7 – 8 and above 8 age groups which constitute 17.63, 12.63 and 7.37 per cent respectively.

Among the women managed units, 3 – 4 and 5 – 6 are the dominant groups which constitute 41.18 and 20.59 per cent respectively, followed by the below 3, 7 – 8 and above 8 age groups which constitute 17.23, 13.02 and 7.98 per cent respectively. Among the jointly managed units, 3 – 4 and below 3 are the dominant groups which constitute 44.23 and 21.15 per cent respectively, followed by the 5 – 6, 7 – 8 and above 8 age groups which constitute 17.31, 11.54 and 5.77 per cent respectively. Among the men managed units, 3 – 4 and 5 – 6 are the dominant groups which constitute 47.37 and

21.05 per cent respectively, followed by the 7 – 8, below 3 and above 8 age groups which constitute 13.16, 10.53 and 7.89 per cent respectively.

4.1.7 Earning Members of the Family

The earning members are the family members who are earning by their own efforts. The number of earning members in the family is an imperative aspect which provides moral and financial support to the respondents. So it is included in the study. The number of earning members of the respondents is grouped into one, two, three, four and more than four. These are illustrated in Table 4.7.

Table 4.7

Earning Members of the Family

S.No	Earning Members of the Family	Number of Respondents			Total
		WMU	JMU	MMU	
1.	One	45 (18.91)	26 (25)	7 (18.42)	78 (20.53)
2.	Two	122 (51.25)	49 (47.12)	16 (42.11)	187 (49.21)
3.	Three	32 (13.45)	17 (16.35)	5 (13.16)	54 (14.21)
4.	Four	31 (13.03)	9 (8.65)	8 (21.05)	48 (12.63)
5.	More than Four	8 (3.36)	3 (2.88)	2 (5.26)	13 (3.42)
	Total	238	104	38	380

Source: Primary data

It is inferred from the above table that two earning members per family and one earning member per family are the dominant groups among the respondents which constitute 49.21 and 20.53 per cent respectively, followed by the three earning members per family, four earning members per family and more than four earning members per family groups which constitute 14.21, 12.63 and 3.42 per cent respectively.

Among the women managed units, two earning members per family and one earning member per family are the dominant groups which constitute 51.25 and 18.91 per cent respectively, followed by the three earning members per family, four earning members per family and more than four earning members per family groups which constitute 13.45, 13.03 and 3.36 per cent respectively. Among the jointly managed units, two earning members per family and one earning member per family are the dominant groups which constitute 47.12 and 25 per cent respectively, followed by the three earning members per family, four earning members per family and more than four earning members per family groups which constitute 16.35, 8.65 and 2.88 per cent respectively. Among the men managed units, two earning members per family and four earning members per family are the dominant groups which constitute 42.11 and 21.05 per cent respectively, followed by the one earning member per family, three earning members per family and more than four earning members per family groups which constitute 18.42, 13.16 and 5.26 per cent respectively.

4.1.8 Personal Income

The personal income of the respondents means the income of the respondents from all possible sources within a period of one month during the study period. The factor of personal income of the respondents not only has its impact on the standard of living, enterprise involvement and constraints but also on the development of their enterprises. So the personal income is included in the study. It has been classified as Rs10000 or less, Rs10001 – Rs15000, Rs15001 – Rs20000, Rs20001 – Rs25000 and more than Rs25000. The distribution of the respondents on the basis of their personal income is shown in table 4.8.

Table 4.8

Personal Income of the Respondents

S.No	Personal Income per month Rs	Number of Respondents			Total
		WMU	JMU	MMU	
1.	10000 or less	38 (15.97)	7 (6.73)	10 (26.32)	55 (14.47)
2.	10001 – 15000	130 (54.62)	10 (9.62)	12 (31.58)	152 (40)
3.	15001 – 20000	38 (15.97)	69 (66.35)	7 (18.42)	114 (30)
4.	20001 – 25000	19 (7.98)	13 (12.5)	4 (10.53)	36 (9.47)
5.	More than 25000	13 (5.46)	5 (4.81)	5 (13.16)	23 (6.05)
	Total	238	104	38	380

Source: Primary data

The above table shows that personal income Rs10001 – Rs15000 per month and personal income Rs15001 – Rs20000 per month are the dominant groups which constitute 40 and 30 per cent respectively, followed by the personal income Rs10000 or less per month, personal income Rs20001 – Rs25000 per month and personal income more than Rs25000 per month groups which constitute 14.47, 9.47 and 6.05 per cent respectively.

Among the women managed units, personal income Rs10001 – Rs15000 per month is the dominant group which constitutes 54.62 per cent followed by the personal income Rs10000 or less per month, personal income Rs15001 – Rs20000 per month, personal income Rs20001 – Rs25000 per month and personal income more than

Rs25000 per month groups which constitute 15.97, 15.97, 7.98 and 5.46 per cent respectively. Among the jointly managed units, personal income Rs15001 – Rs20000 per month and personal income Rs20001 – Rs25000 per month are the dominant groups which constitute 66.35 and 12.5 per cent respectively, followed by the personal income Rs10001 – Rs15000 per month, personal income Rs10000 or less per month and personal income more than Rs25000 per month groups which constitute 9.62, 6.73 and 4.81 per cent respectively. Among the men managed units, personal income Rs10001 – Rs15000 per month and personal income Rs10000 or less per month are the dominant groups which constitute 31.58 and 26.32 per cent respectively, followed by the personal income Rs15001 – Rs20000 per month, personal income more than Rs25000 per month and personal income Rs20001 – Rs25000 per month groups which constitute 18.42, 13.16 and 10.53 per cent respectively.

4.1.9 Occupational Background of the Respondents

The occupational background represents the occupation of the parents or husband or anybody else on which the respondent was dependent once before starting the enterprise. The occupational background provides the financial development and moral support to the respondents. The occupational backgrounds taken into consideration are labourer, farmer, government employee, private employee and entrepreneur. The distribution of the respondents on the basis of occupational background is exhibited in table 4.9.

Table 4.9

Occupational Background of the Respondents

S.No	Occupational Background	Number of Respondents			Total
		WMU	JMU	MMU	
1.	Labourer	18 (7.56)	4 (3.85)	5 (13.16)	27 (7.11)
2.	Farmer	32 (13.45)	14 (13.46)	5 (13.16)	51 (13.42)
3.	Government Employee	55 (23.11)	17 (16.35)	7 (18.42)	79 (20.79)
4.	Private Employee	64 (26.89)	32 (30.77)	12 (31.58)	108 (28.42)
5.	Entrepreneur	69 (28.99)	37 (35.59)	9 (23.68)	115 (30.26)
	Total	**238**	**104**	**38**	**380**

Source: Primary data

It is revealed from the above table that most of the respondents are entrepreneurs and private employees who constitute 30.26 and 28.42 per cent respectively, followed by government employees, farmers and labourer who constitute 20.79, 13.42 and 7.11 per cent respectively.

Among the women managed units, most of the respondents are entrepreneurs and private employees who constitute 28.99 and 26.89 per cent respectively, followed by government employees, farmers and labourer who constitute 23.11, 13.45 and 7.56 per cent respectively. Among the jointly managed units, most of the respondents are entrepreneurs and private employees who constitute 35.59 and 30.77 per cent respectively, followed by government employees, farmers and labourer who constitute 16.35, 13.46 and 3.85 per cent respectively. Among the men managed units, most of the respondents are private employees and entrepreneurs who constitute 31.58 and

23.68 per cent respectively, followed by government employees, farmers and labourer who constitute 18.42, 13.16 and 13.16 per cent respectively.

4.1.10 Position before Starting the Enterprise of the Respondents

The experience of the respondents before starting their enterprises plays a vital role for the development of the enterprise. Since the previous position the respondents before starting their enterprises acts as a foundation stone to build a new enterprise, it is included in the study. It is confined to student, unemployed, employed, house wife and in another enterprise. The distribution of the respondents on the basis of position before starting the enterprise is exhibited in table 4.10.

Table 4.10

Position before Starting the Enterprise of the Respondents

S.No	Position	Number of Respondents			Total
		WMU	JMU	MMU	
1.	Student	22 (9.24)	10 (9.62)	13 (34.21)	45 (11.84)
2.	Unemployed	38 (15.97)	21 (20.19)	12 (31.58)	71 (18.68)
3.	Employed	16 (6.72)	19 (18.27)	4 (10.53)	39 (10.26)
4.	House Wife	151 (63.45)	46 (44.23)	6 (15.79)	203 (53.42)
5.	In Another Enterprise	11 (4.62)	8 (7.69)	3 (7.89)	22 (5.79)
	Total	**238**	**104**	**38**	**380**

Source: Primary data

It is clearly seen from the above table that the many of the respondents were house wives who constitute 53.42 per cent, followed by the group of unemployed, student, employed and in another enterprise that constitute 18.68, 11.84, 10.26 and 5.79 per cent respectively.

Among the women managed units, house wives form the dominant group which constitutes 63.45 per cent, followed by unemployed, student, employed and in another enterprise which constitute 15.97, 9.24, 6.72 and 4.62 per cent respectively. Among the jointly managed units, once again the house wives form the dominant group which constitutes 44.23 per cent, followed by unemployed, employed, student and in another enterprise which constitute 20.19, 18.27, 9.62 and 7.69 per cent respectively. Among the men managed units, student and unemployed are the dominant groups which constitute 34.21 and 31.58 per cent respectively, followed by house wives, employed and in another enterprise groups which constitute 15.79, 10.53 and 7.89 per cent respectively.

4.1.11 Occasion of the Training Programme of the Respondents

Occasion of the training programme of the respondents means the time of participation of the respondents in the training programme for the purpose of gathering knowledge and ideas regarding enterprises concerned. Since the participation time helps the entrepreneurs for their development, it is included in the study. This is classified into five categories, namely, before starting the enterprise, at the time of starting the enterprise, after starting the enterprise, before and after starting the enterprise and no training so far. The distribution of the respondents on the occasion of the training programme is exhibited in table 4.11.

Table 4.11

Occasion of the Training Programme of the Respondents

S.No	Occasion of the Training	Number of Respondents			Total
		WMU	JMU	MMU	
1.	Before Starting the Enterprise	57 (23.95)	19 (18.27)	10 (26.31)	86 (22.63)
2.	At the Time of Starting the Enterprise	29 (12.18)	10 (9.62)	4 (10.53)	43 (11.32)
3.	After Starting the Enterprise	38 (15.97)	18 (17.31)	8 (21.05)	64 (16.84)
4.	Before and After Starting the Enterprise	19 (7.98)	10 (9.62)	5 (13.16)	34 (8.95)
5.	No Training so far	95 (39.92)	47 (45.18)	11 (28.95)	153 (40.26)
	Total	238	104	38	380

Source: Primary data

The above table reveals that 40.26 per cent of respondents did not undergo any training so far, followed by the respondents who attended the programme, before starting the enterprises, after starting the enterprises, at the time of starting the enterprises and before and after starting the enterprises which constitute 22.63, 16.84, 11.32 and 8.95 per cent respectively.

Among the women managed units, 39.92 per cent of respondents did not undergo any training so far, followed by the respondents who attended the programme, before starting the enterprises, after starting the enterprises, at the time of starting the enterprises and before and after starting the enterprises who constitute 23.95, 15.97,

12.18 and 7.98 per cent respectively. Among the jointly managed units, 45.18 per cent of respondents did not undergo any training so far, followed by the respondents who attended the programme, before starting the enterprises, after starting the enterprises, at the time of starting the enterprises and before and after starting the enterprises who constitute 18.27, 17.31, 9.62 and 9.62 per cent respectively. Among the men managed units, 28.95 per cent of respondents did not undergo any training so far, followed by the respondents who attended the programme, before starting the enterprises, after starting the enterprises, at the time of starting the enterprises and before and after starting the enterprises who constitute 26.31, 21.05, 13.16 and 10.53 per cent respectively.

4.2 DESCRIPTIVE ANALYSIS OF THE ORGANIZATIONAL PROFILE

Organization represents the units run by the respondents in the present study. The profile of the organization may have its impact on the performance of the organization. Nirmala Karuna D'Cruz (2003) studied the enterprise profile in her study and categorized it as type of enterprise (individual or group activity), nature of enterprise (proprietary, co-operative, or trust), date of registration, capital investment, financial development assistance availed, incentives, awards received, recognition received, growth rate (in terms of increase in value of sales, number of employees, and value of assets development), and diversification carried out. Even though, the profiles of the organization are too many, the present study confines to the following variables: nature of enterprise, types of sector, number of employee, enterprise premise, age of enterprise, monthly turnover, monthly profit, mode of creation, time of registration and membership in association.

4.2.1 Nature of the Enterprise

The nature of the enterprise indicates the direction of enterprise among the units. In general, the nature of enterprise is classified on the basis of the nature of work done by the enterprise unit. It is classified into manufacturing, repairing & maintenance, trading, services and others. The selection of enterprises related to different lines rests on the capability, opportunity and interest among the entrepreneurs. The selection of the field of enterprise may show its own impact on the performance. Hence, the present study includes the nature of enterprise as one of the profile variables of the organization. The nature of enterprise in the present study is confined to manufacturing, repairing & maintenance, trading, services and others. The distribution of the respondents on the basis of the nature of enterprise is shown in table 4.12.

Table 4.12

Nature of the Enterprise

S.No	Nature of the Enterprise	Number of Respondents			Total
		WMU	JMU	MMU	
1.	Manufacturing	48 (20.17)	42 (40.38)	8 (21.05)	98 (25.79)
2.	Repairing and Maintenance	57 (23.95)	17 (16.35)	5 (13.15)	79 (20.79)
3.	Trading	38 (15.97)	12 (11.54)	10 (26.32)	60 (15.79)
4.	Services	67 (28.15)	24 (23.08)	11 (28.95)	102 (26.84)
5.	Others	28 (11.76)	9 (8.65)	4 (10.53)	41 (10.79)
	Total	238	104	38	380

Source: Primary data

The above table reveals that most of the respondents go for services and manufacturing that constitute 26.84 and 25.79 per cent respectively and 20.79, 15.79 and 10.79 per cent of the respondents go for repairing and maintenance, trading and others respectively.

Among the women managed units, 28.15 and 23.95 per cent of the respondents go for services and repairing and maintenance respectively and 20.17, 15.97 and 11.76 per cent of the respondents go for manufacturing, trading and others respectively. Among the jointly managed units, 40.38 and 23.08 per cent of the respondents involve themselves in manufacturing and services respectively whereas 16.35, 11.54 and 8.65 per cent of the respondents involve themselves in repairing and maintenance, trading and others respectively. Among the men managed units, 28.95 and 26.32 per cent of the respondents involve themselves in service and trading respectively whereas 21.05, 13.15 and 10.53 per cent of the respondents involve themselves in manufacturing, repairing and maintenance and others respectively.

4.2.2 Types of the Sector of the Enterprises

The types of sector of the enterprises indicate the direction of nature of enterprise among the units. In general, types of the sector of the enterprises are classified on the basis of the type of work done by the enterprise unit. It is classified into garments, textile & tailoring, printing & computer based jobs, beauty parlour, dairy farming & poultry and others. The selection of the types of the sector of the enterprises may have its own impact on the performance. Hence, the present study includes the types of the sector of the enterprises as one of the profile variables of the organization. The types of the sector of the enterprise in the present study are confined to garments, textile & tailoring, printing & computer based jobs, beauty parlour, dairy farming & poultry and others. The distribution of the respondents on the basis of the types of sector of the enterprises is shown in table 4.13.

Table 4.13

Types of the Sector of the Enterprises

S.No	Type of Sector	Number of Respondents			Total
		WMU	JMU	MMU	
1.	Garments , Textile & Tailoring	57 (23.95)	28 (26.92)	10 (26.32)	95 (25)
2.	Printing & Computer based Jobs	105 (44.12)	38 (36.54)	13 (34.21)	156 (41.05)
3.	Beauty Parlour	10 (4.2)	10 (9.62)	4 (10.53)	24 (6.32)
4.	Dairy Farming & Poultry	28 (11.76)	18 (17.30)	5 (13.16)	51 (13.42)
5.	Others	38 (15.97)	10 (9.62)	6 (15.78)	54 (14.21)
	Total	**238**	**104**	**38**	**380**

Source: Primary data

The above table reveals that 41.05 and 25 per cent of the respondents have chosen printing & computer based jobs and garments, textile & tailoring respectively, whereas sectors like other type, others, dairy farming & poultry and beauty parlour are chosen by 14.21, 13.42 and 6.32 per cent of the respondents respectively.

Among the women managed units, 44.12 and 23.95 per cent of the respondents involve themselves in printing & computer based jobs and garments, textile & tailoring respectively and 15.97, 11.76 and 4.2 per cent of the respondents involve themselves in others, dairy farming & poultry and beauty parlour respectively. Among the jointly managed units, 36.54 and 26.92 per cent of the respondents involve themselves in printing & computer based jobs and garments, textile & tailoring respectively and dairy 17.30, 9.62 and 9.62 per cent of the respondents involve themselves in farming & poultry, beauty parlour and others respectively. Among the men managed units, 34.21

and 26.32 per cent of the respondents involve themselves in printing & computer based jobs and garments, textile & tailoring respectively and 15.78, 13.16 and 10.53 per cent of the respondents involve themselves in others, dairy farming & poultry and beauty parlour respectively.

4.2.3 Number of Employees

Entrepreneurship provides employment opportunity to many. In the small scale industries, employment opportunity is visible. In order to analyze this aspect, the number of employees engaged in enterprise units have been taken into account and classified as 1 – 3, 4 – 6, 7 – 9, 10 – 12 and above 12. The distribution of the respondents on the basis of the number of employee of the enterprise is shown in table 4.14.

Table 4.14

Number of Employees of the Enterprise

S.No	Number of Employees	Number of Respondents			Total
		WMU	JMU	MMU	
1.	1 – 3	6 (2.52)	3 (2.88)	2 (5.26)	11 (2.89)
2.	4 – 6	24 (10.08)	7 (6.73)	9 (23.68)	40 (10.53)
3.	7 – 9	46 (19.33)	18 (17.31)	13 (34.22)	77 (20.26)
4.	10 – 12	102 (42.86)	27 (25.96)	11 (28.95)	140 (36.85)
5.	Above 12	60 (25.21)	49 (47.12)	3 (7.89)	112 (29.47)
	Total	238	104	38	380

Source: Primary data

The above table reveals that 36.85 and 29.47 per cent of the respondents have 10 – 12 and above 12 numbers of employees respectively and 20.26, 10.53 and 2.89 per cent of the respondents have 7 – 9, 4 – 6 and 1 – 3 numbers of employees respectively.

Among the women managed units, 42.86 and 25.21 per cent of the respondents have 10 – 12 and above 12 numbers of employees respectively and 19.33, 10.08 and 2.52 per cent of the respondents have 7 – 9, 4 – 6 and 1 – 3 numbers of employees respectively. Among the jointly managed units, 47.12 and 25.96 per cent of the respondents have above 12 and 10 – 12 numbers of employees respectively and 17.31, 6.73 and 2.88 per cent of the respondents have 7 – 9, 4 – 6 and 1 – 3 numbers of employees respectively. Among the men managed units, 34.22 and 28.95 per cent of the respondents have 7 – 9 and 10 – 12 numbers of employees respectively and 23.68, 7.89 and 5.26 per cent of the respondents have 4 – 6, above 12 and 1 – 3 numbers of employees respectively.

4.2.4   Nature of Premises of the Enterprise

Nature of premises of the enterprise of the respondents indicates the exact place where the enterprise is run by the respondents at the time of study period. Since the location of the enterprise plays a vital role for the development of the entrepreneurs, it is included in the study. Nature of premises of the enterprise of the respondents are classified as owned, partially owned, rented, leased and others. The distribution of the nature of premises of the enterprise of the respondents is shown in table 4.15.

Table 4.15

Nature of Premises of the Enterprise

S.No	Nature of Premises	Number of Respondents			Total
		WMU	JMU	MMU	
1.	Owned	82 (34.45)	48 (46.75)	13 (34.21)	143 (37.63)
2.	Partially Owned	27 (11.34)	9 (8.65)	7 (18.42)	43 (11.32)
3.	Rented	67 (28.15)	28 (26.92)	12 (31.58)	107 (28.16)
4.	Leased	43 (18.06)	14 (13.46)	4 (10.53)	61 (16.05)
5.	Others	19 (7.98)	5 (4.81)	2 (5.26)	26 (6.84)
	Total	238	104	38	380

Source: Primary data

The above table reveals that 37.63 per cent of the respondents have their own premises, 28.16 per cent of the respondents have rented premises, 16.05 per cent of the respondents have leased premises, 11.32 per cent of the respondents have partially owned premises and 6.84 per cent of the respondents have others type of premises.

Among the women managed units, 34.45, 28.15, 18.06, 11.34 and 7.98 per cent of the respondents have owned, rented, leased, partially owned and others respectively. Among the jointly managed units, 46.75, 26.92, 13.46, 8.65 and 4.81 per cent of the respondents have owned, rented, leased, partially owned and others respectively. Among the men managed units, 34.21, 31.58, 18.42, 10.53 and 5.26 per cent of the respondents have owned, rented, partially owned, leased and others respectively.

4.2.5 Age of Enterprise

Age of enterprise represents the number of years of the enterprise of the respondents. Since the age of enterprise of the respondents may have its impact on enterprising, it is included in the present study. The more age an enterprise has, it will expose more knowledge in its trade and it will manage the business well. Consequently, its performance in the respective enterprise will be enriched. In the present study, the age of enterprise among the respondents are confined to below 1 year, 1 – 5 years, 6 – 10 years, 11 – 15 years and above 15 years. 'The distribution of the respondents on the basis of age of enterprise is presented below in table 4.16.

Table 4.16

Age of Enterprise

S.No	Age of Enterprise	Number of Respondents			Total
		WMU	JMU	MMU	
1.	Below 1 year	25 (10.5)	13 (12.5)	7 (18.42)	45 (11.84)
2.	1 – 5 years	118 (49.58)	48 (46.15)	12 (31.58)	178 (46.84)
3.	6 – 10 years	44 (18.49)	24 (23.08)	11 (28.95)	79 (20.79)
4.	11 – 15 years	31 (13.03)	11 (10.58)	5 (13.16)	47 (12.37)
5.	Above 15 years	20 (8.4)	8 (7.69)	3 (7.89)	31 (8.16)
	Total	**238**	**104**	**38**	**380**

The above table reveals that the dominant groups among the respondents are 1 – 5 years and 6 – 10 years which constitute 46.84 and 20.79 per cent respectively, followed by the groups of 11 – 15 years, below 1 year and above 15 years which constitute 12.37, 11.84 and 8.16 per cent respectively.

Among the women managed units, the dominant groups are 1 – 5 years and 6 – 10 years which constitute 49.58 and 18.49 per cent respectively, followed by the groups of 11 – 15 years, below 1 year and above 15 years which constitutes 13.03, 10.5 and 8.4 per cent respectively. Among the jointly managed units, the dominant groups are 1 – 5 years and 6 – 10 years which constitute 46.15 and 23.08 per cent respectively, followed by the groups of below 1 year, 11 – 15 years and above 15 years which constitutes 12.5, 10.58 and 7.69 per cent respectively. Among the men managed units, the dominant groups are 1 – 5 years and 6 – 10 years which constitute 31.58 and 28.95 per cent respectively followed by the groups of below 1 year, 11 – 15 years and above 15 years which constitutes 18.42, 13.16 and 7.89 per cent respectively.

4.2.6 Monthly Turnover

Monthly turnover in the present study represents the sales turnover achieved by the respondent per month during the study period. The sales turnover is one of the important factors which determine the ability of the enterprise regarding its performance. It also shows the marketability of the unit. In the present study, the monthly turnover is classified as Rs1 lakh or less, above Rs1 – Rs3 lakh, above Rs3 – Rs5 lakh, above Rs5 – Rs7 lakh and above Rs7 lakh. The distribution of the respondents according to their monthly turnover achieved in their enterprises is illustrated in table 4.17.

Table 4.17

Monthly Turnover of the Enterprise

S.No	Monthly Turnover Rs	Number of Respondents			Total
		WMU	JMU	MMU	
1.	1 lakh or less	46 (19.33)	25 (24.04)	10 (26.32)	81 (21.32)
2.	Above 1 – 3 lakh	88 (36.97)	42 (40.38)	12 (31.58)	142 (37.37)
3.	Above 3 – 5 lakh	49 (20.59)	18 (17.31)	8 (21.05)	75 (19.74)
4.	Above 5 – 7 lakh	36 (15.13)	13 (12.5)	5 (13.16)	54 (14.21)
5.	Above 7 lakh	19 (7.98)	6 (5.77)	3 (7.89)	28 (7.37)
	Total	238	104	38	380

Source: Primary data

The above table reveals that the dominant groups among the respondents are above Rs1 – Rs3 lakh and 1 lakh or less which constitute 37.37 and 21.32 per cent respectively, followed by the groups of above Rs2 – Rs5 lakh, above Rs5 – Rs7 lakh and above Rs7 lakh which constitute 19.74, 14.21 and 7.37 per cent respectively.

Among the women managed units, the dominant groups are above Rs1 – Rs3 lakh and above Rs3 – Rs5 lakh which constitute 36.97 and 20.59 per cent respectively, followed by the groups of Rs1 lakh or less, above Rs5 – Rs7 lakh and above Rs7 lakh which constitute 19.33, 15.13 and 7.98 per cent respectively. Among the jointly managed units, the dominant groups are above Rs1 – Rs3 lakh and Rs1 lakh or less which constitute 40.38 and 24.04 per cent respectively, followed by the groups of above Rs3 – Rs5 lakh, above Rs5 – Rs7 lakh and above Rs7 lakh which constitute 17.31, 12.5 and 5.77 per cent respectively. Among the men managed units, the dominant groups are above Rs1 – Rs3 lakh and Rs1 lakh or less which constitute 31.58 and 26.32 per cent respectively, followed by the groups of above Rs3 – Rs5 lakh, above Rs5 – Rs7 lakh and above Rs7 lakh which constitute 21.05, 13.16 and 7.89 per cent respectively.

4.2.7 Monthly Profit

Monthly profit is the difference between the total revenue realized in the enterprise and the expenses incurred in the enterprise. All entrepreneurs aim at maximum profit. They want to increase their profit consistently. Since profit is one of the important measuring yards of the performance of the unit, it is included in the present study. The monthly profits are classified as Rs10000 or less, Rs10001 to Rs20000, Rs20001 to Rs30000, Rs30001 to Rs40000 and above Rs40000. The distribution of the respondents according to their monthly profit achieved in their enterprise is illustrated in table 4.18.

Table 4.18
Monthly Profit of the Enterprise

S.No	Monthly Profit Rs	Number of Respondents			Total
		WMU	JMU	MMU	
1.	10,000 or less	35 (14.71)	15 (14.42)	9 (23.68)	59 (15.53)
2.	10,001 – 20,000	46 (19.33)	43 (41.35)	14 (36.84)	103 (27.11)
3.	20,001 – 30,000	105 (44.12)	31 (29.81)	7 (18.42)	143 (37.63)
4.	30,001 – 40,000	28 (11.76)	11 (10.58)	6 (15.79)	45 (11.84)
5.	Above 40,000	24 (10.08)	4 (3.85)	2 (5.26)	30 (7.89)
	Total	238	104	38	380

Source: Primary data

The above table reveals that the dominant groups among the respondents are Rs20,001 – Rs30,000 and Rs10,001 – Rs20,000 which constitute 37.63 and 27.11 per cent respectively, followed by the groups of Rs10,000 or less, Rs30,001 – Rs40,000 and above Rs40,000 which constitute 15.53, 11.84 and 7.89 per cent respectively.

Among the women managed units, the dominant groups are Rs20,001 – Rs30,000 and Rs10,001 – Rs20,000 which constitute 44.12 and 19.33 per cent respectively, followed by the groups of Rs10,000 or less, Rs30,001 – Rs40,000 and above Rs40,000 which constitute 14.71, 11.76 and 10.08 per cent respectively. Among the jointly managed units, the dominant groups are Rs10,001 – Rs20,000 and Rs20,001 – Rs30,000 which constitute 41.35 and 29.81 per cent respectively, followed by the groups of Rs10,000 or less, Rs30,001 – Rs40,000 and above Rs40,000 which constitute 14.42, 10.58 and 3.85 per cent respectively. Among the men managed units, the dominant groups are Rs10,001 – Rs20,000 and Rs10,000 or less which constitute 36.84 and 23.68 per cent respectively, followed by the groups of Rs20,001 – Rs30,000, Rs30,001 – Rs40,000 and above Rs40,000 which constitute 18.42, 15.79 and 5.26 per cent respectively.

4.2.8 Mode of Creation

Mode of creation means the way in which the respondents created their enterprises. It is purely related to the psychological factor which leads to the degree of development of their enterprise. Since the mode of creation has an important role in the development of the enterprise of the respondents, it is included in the study. Mode of creation has been classified as enterprise created by self, family enterprise (Inherited), enterprise which has been bought, leased and others. The distribution of the respondents according to the mode of creation of their enterprises is illustrated in table 4.19.

Table 4.19

Mode of Creation of the Enterprise

S.No	Mode of Creation	Number of Respondents			Total
		WMU	JMU	MMU	
1.	Enterprise Created by self	94 (39.50)	39 (37.5)	14 (36.84)	147 (38.68)
2.	Family Enterprise (Inherited)	38 (15.97)	24 (23.08)	7 (18.42)	69 (18.16)
3.	Enterprise which has been Bought	72 (30.25)	37 (35.58)	9 (23.68)	118 (31.05)
4.	Leased	25 (10.50)	3 (2.88)	6 (15.79)	34 (8.95)
5.	Others	9 (3.78)	1 (0.96)	2 (5.26)	12 (3.16)
	Total	238	104	38	380

Source: Primary data

The above table reveals that the dominant groups among the respondents are enterprise created by self and enterprise which has been bought which constitute 38.68 and 31.05 per cent respectively, followed by the groups of family enterprise (Inherited), leased and others which constitute 18.16, 8.95 and 3.16 per cent respectively.

Among the women managed units, the dominant groups are enterprise created by self and enterprise which has been bought which constitute 39.50 and 30.25 per cent respectively, followed by the groups of family enterprise (Inherited), leased and others which constitute 15.97, 10.50 and 3.78 per cent respectively. Among the jointly managed units, the dominant groups are enterprise created by self and enterprise which has been bought which constitute 37.5 and 35.58 per cent respectively, followed by the groups of family enterprise (Inherited), leased and others which constitute 23.08, 2.88 and 0.96 per cent respectively. Among the men managed units, the dominant groups are enterprise created by self and enterprise which has been bought which constitute 36.84 and 23.68 per cent respectively, followed by the groups of family enterprise (Inherited), leased and others which constitute 18.42, 15.79 and 5.26 per cent respectively.

4.2.9 Time of Registration in DIC

Time of registration in the District Industries Centre indicates the occasion of the registration of the enterprise of the respondents in the District Industries Centre. District Industries Centre is a government organization under the control of the department of Industries and Commerce which promotes and provides facilitation to the enterprises throughout their lifecycles aiming for industrialization of the district and thereby creating employment generation to the masses. The District Industries Centre acts as a junction for the entrepreneurs for seeking information, gathering knowledge, sharing experience, avoiding constraints, getting government support and necessary training. Since the time of registration of the enterprise of the respondents in the District Industries Centre is very essential for the development of their enterprises, it is included in the study. The time of registration is categorized as i) after starting the enterprise, ii) at the time of starting the enterprise, iii) at the time of bank loan, iv) before starting the enterprise and v) not yet registered. The distribution of the respondents according to the time of registration of the enterprise is illustrated in table 4.20.

Table 4.20

Time of Registration in DIC

S.No	Time of Registration	Number of Respondents			Total
		WMU	JMU	MMU	
1.	After Starting the Enterprise	47 (19.75)	26 (25)	8 (21.05)	81 (21.32)
2.	At the time of Starting the Enterprise	38 (15.97)	17 (16.35)	9 (23.68)	64 (16.84)
3.	At the time of Bank Loan	65 (27.31)	39 (15.38)	13 (34.21)	117 (30.79)
4.	Before Starting the Enterprise	26 (10.92)	15 (14.42)	5 (13.16)	46 (12.11)
5.	Not yet Registered	62 (26.05)	7 (6.73)	3 (7.89)	72 (18.95)
	Total	**238**	**104**	**38**	**380**

Source: Primary data

The above table reveals that 30.79 per cent of the respondents registered their enterprises at the time of bank loan, 21.32 per cent per cent of the respondents registered their enterprises after starting the enterprise, 18.95 per cent of the respondents not registered their enterprises so far, 16.84 per cent of the respondents registered their enterprises at the time of starting the enterprise and 12.11 per cent per cent of the respondents registered their enterprises before starting the enterprise respectively.

Among the women managed units, the dominant groups are at the time of bank loan and not yet registered which constitute 27.31 and 26.05 per cent respectively, followed by the groups of after started the enterprise, at the time of starting the enterprise and before starting the enterprise which constitute 19.75, 15.97 and 10.92 per cent respectively. Among the jointly managed units, the dominant groups are after started the enterprise and at the time of starting the enterprise which constitute 25 and 16.35 per cent respectively, followed by the groups of at the time of bank loan, before starting the enterprise and not yet registered which constitute, 15.38, 14.42 and 6.73 per cent respectively. Among the men managed units, the dominant groups are at the time of bank loan and at the time of starting the enterprise which constitute 34.21 and 23.68 per cent respectively, followed by the groups of after started the enterprise, before starting the enterprise and not yet registered which constitute 21.05, 13.16 and 7.89 per cent respectively.

4.2.10 Membership in Association

Membership in association of the respondents indicates the membership of the respondents in any related association which may be government or non government. Some of the activities of the association are advertising, education, political donations, lobbying and publishing, but its main focus is collaboration between companies, or standardization. Associations may offer other services, such as organizing conferences, networking or charitable events or offering classes or educational materials. Many associations are non-profit organizations governed by bylaws and directed by officers who are also members. Since the membership in an association of the respondents is a also key factor for the development of their enterprises, it is included in the study. Membership in association is categorized as related trade association, local association, association of women entrepreneurs, self help groups and none. The distribution of the respondents according to the membership in association is illustrated in table 4.21.

Table 4.21

Membership in Association of the Respondents

S.No	Membership	Number of Respondents			Total
		WMU	JMU	MMU	
1.	Related Trade Association	112 (47.06)	37 (35.58)	13 (34.21)	162 (42.63)
2.	Local Association	47 (19.75)	35 (33.65)	11 (28.95)	93 (24.47)
3.	Association of Women Entrepreneurs	33 (13.87)	22 (21.15)	7 (18.42)	62 (16.32)
4.	Self Help Groups	28 (11.76)	6 (5.77)	5 (13.16)	39 (10.26)
5.	None	18 (7.56)	4 (3.85)	2 (5.26)	24 (6.32)
	Total	238	104	38	380

Source: Primary data

The above table reveals that the dominant groups among the respondents are related trade association and local association which constitute 42.63 and 24.47 per cent respectively, followed by the groups of association of women entrepreneurs, self help groups and none which constitute 16.32, 10.26 and 6.32 per cent respectively.

Among the women managed units, the dominant group are related trade association and local association which constitute 47.06 and 19.75 per cent respectively, followed by the groups of association of women entrepreneurs, self help groups and none which constitute 13.87, 11.76 and 7.56 per cent respectively. Among the jointly managed units, the dominant groups are related trade association and local association which constitute 35.58 and 33.65 per cent respectively, followed by the groups of association of women entrepreneurs, self help groups and none which constitute 21.15, 5.77 and 3.85 per cent respectively. Among the men managed units, the dominant groups are related trade association and local association which constitute 34.21 and 28.95 per cent respectively, followed by the groups of association of women entrepreneurs, self help groups and none which constitute 18.42, 13.16 and 5.26 per cent respectively.

CHAPTER V

ANALYSIS AND INTERPRETATIONS OF VARIOUS DEVELOPMENTS

This chapter deals with the analysis and interpretations of the developments of various variables and factors such as personality development, social development, personal development, innovational development, embankment development and intellectual development of the respondents in Tirunelveli district. The development of various variables and categories of the respondents is done in the first part and the development on various factors of the respondents is done in the later part of the chapter. One-Sample t Test and Factor analysis have been used to analyze the developments of women entrepreneurs and to draw inferences.

The One-Sample t Test procedure, tests whether the mean of a single variable differs from a specified constant. The mean value is displayed in the One-Sample Statistics table, and the constant of test value displayed in the One-Sample t test table. The table consists of mean, standard deviation, t value, P value, the average difference between each data value and the hypothesized test value, a confidence interval for this difference for each test variable. A low significance value (typically below 0.05) indicates that there is a significant difference between the test value and the observed mean. If the confidence interval for the mean difference does not contain zero, this also indicates that the difference is significant. If the significance value is high, negative and the confidence interval for the mean difference contains zero, then it cannot conclude that there is a significant difference between the test value and the observed mean. Since the One-Sample t Test procedure compares the mean to a specified value, it is useful to know what the mean value is.

5.1 One-Sample t Test of the Developments of Women Entrepreneurs

The One-Sample t Test procedure is used here to find out whether any specific development occurs in various development variables of women entrepreneurs and in various categories of women entrepreneurs when compare to the average level. Test value was fixed as 10 based on the average mean of a subject who can score maximum 20 for a variable. In the study totally forty variables are selected under the head of the factors such as personality development, social development, personal development, innovational development, embankment development and intellectual development to find out the developments of women entrepreneurs. The personality development factor consist of seven variables such as planning, information seeking, problem solving, confidence, honesty, faithfulness and persuasiveness. The social development factor consist of six variables such as positive environment, social and family responsibilities, decreasing social barriers, women business network, administrative and legal support, and admiration at public places. The personal development factor consists of seven variables such as assets development, financial development, workplace development, environmental development, marketplace development, values development and managerial skill development. The innovational development factor consists of seven variables such as low margin, more sales & more profit, best quality production, effective communication and negotiation skills, advertisement, discount & prizes, prompt delivery & supply and preparing action plan. The embankment development factors consists of seven variables such as money transaction through bank, using bank loan with subsidy, direct approach to the bank officials, avoiding mediators for loan, prompt repayment of the loan, regular contact with bank officials and using mobile banking. The intellectual development factor consists of six variables such as internet usage, prompt communication, accounting & auditing, budget preparation, examining the business network and computerized work.

HYPOTHESIS I

Null Hypothesis: There is no significant development on the selected variables of women entrepreneurs compare to the average level (Mean = 10)

Table 5.1

One-Sample t Test of the Variables of Development Factors

Variables	Test Value = 10					95% Confidence Interval of the Diff.	
	Mean	SD	t value	P value	Mean Diff.	Lower	Upper
Planning	15.18	4.883	20.696	.000**	5.18	4.69	5.68
Information Seeking	14.97	4.182	23.181	.000**	4.97	4.55	5.39

Problem Solving	14.61	4.458	20.139	.000**	4.61	4.16	5.05
Confidence	14.42	4.428	19.461	.000**	4.42	3.97	4.87
Honesty	14.58	4.338	20.576	.000**	4.58	4.14	5.02
Faithfulness	13.97	4.445	17.425	.000**	3.97	3.53	4.42
Persuasiveness	13.89	4.465	17.004	.000**	3.89	3.44	4.35
Positive Environment	10.95	5.298	03.486	.001**	0.95	0.41	1.48
Social and Family Responsibilities	11.59	5.353	05.798	.000**	1.59	1.05	2.13
Decreasing Social Barriers	10.89	5.377	03.244	.001**	0.89	0.35	1.44
Women Business Network	08.92	4.982	-4.222	.000**	-1.08	-1.58	-0.58
Administrative and Legal Support	09.08	4.654	-3.858	.000**	-0.92	-1.39	-0.45
Admiration at Public Places	09.16	5.114	-3.210	.001**	-0.84	-1.36	-0.33
Assets Development	08.88	4.138	-5.256	.000**	-1.12	-1.53	-0.70
Financial Development	10.96	4.937	03.772	.000**	0.96	0.46	1.45
Workplace Development	11.47	4.718	06.089	.000**	1.47	0.99	1.95
Environmental development	11.66	4.596	07.032	.000**	1.66	1.19	2.12
Marketplace Development	11.39	4.717	05.765	.000**	1.39	0.92	1.87
Values Development	13.24	4.902	12.871	.000**	3.24	2.74	3.73
Managerial Skill Development	11.76	4.475	07.681	.000**	1.76	1.31	2.21
Low Margin, More Sales & More Profit	10.50	5.109	01.908	.057	0.50	0.11	0.89
Best Quality Production	13.50	4.622	14.763	.000**	3.50	3.03	3.97

Effective Communication and Negotiation Skills	12.42	4.833	09.765	.000**	2.42	1.93	2.91
Advertisement	13.03	4.201	14.042	.000**	3.03	2.60	3.45
Discount & Prizes	10.89	4.707	03.706	.000**	0.89	0.42	1.37
Prompt Delivery & Supply	12.89	4.707	11.989	.000**	2.89	2.42	3.37
Preparing Action Plan	10.74	4.259	03.373	.001**	0.74	0.31	1.17
Money Transaction through Bank	11.11	3.156	06.826	.000**	1.11	0.79	1.42
Using Bank Loan with Subsidy	15.89	3.287	34.955	.000**	5.89	5.56	6.23
Direct Approach to the Bank Officials	09.50	4.429	-2.201	.052	-0.50	-0.95	-0.05
Avoiding Mediators for Loan	09.21	4.965	-3.100	.002**	-0.79	-1.29	-0.29
Prompt Repayment of the Loan	16.95	2.718	49.835	.000**	6.95	6.67	7.22
Regular Contact with Bank Officials	10.03	4.099	00.125	.900	0.03	0.01	0.05
Using Mobile Banking	08.89	4.558	-4.726	.000**	-1.11	-1.57	-0.65
Internet Usage	10.11	4.069	00.504	.614	0.11	0.05	0.15
Prompt Communication	13.42	4.598	14.504	.000**	3.42	2.96	3.88
Accounting & Auditing	11.63	4.699	06.769	.000**	1.63	1.16	2.10
Budget Preparation	09.90	4.419	-0.430	.668	-0.10	-0.54	-0.35
Examining the Business Network	13.68	4.623	15.533	.000**	3.68	3.22	4.15
Computerized Work	10.50	4.778	2.040	.052	0.50	0.02	0.98

**Significant at .05 level of confidence

Since P value is less than 0.05, the null hypothesis is rejected at 5 % level of significance with regard to the variables of planning, information seeking, problem solving, confidence, honesty, faithfulness, persuasiveness, positive environment, social and family responsibilities, decreasing social barriers, financial developments, workplace developments, environmental developments, marketplace developments, values developments, managerial skill developments, best quality production, effective communication and negotiation skills, advertisement, discount & prizes, prompt delivery & supply, preparing action plan, money transaction through bank, using bank loan scheme with subsidy, prompt repayment of the loan, prompt communication, accounting & auditing and examining the business network of the development of women entrepreneurs. Hence, the developments level of women entrepreneurs is higher than the average level (Mean = 10). The mean of these variables is more than 10 which clearly demonstrates that the development level of women entrepreneurs is significantly higher than the average level. Besides the mean of some variables is below the average level (Mean = 10) as shown in the above table.

Since P value is higher than 0.05, the null hypothesis is failed to reject at 5 % level of significance with regard to the variables of low margin, more sales & more profit, direct approach to the bank officials, regular contact with bank officials, internet usage, budget preparation and computerized work of the development of women entrepreneurs.

Even though there is a statistical difference in the variables of women business network, administrative and legal support, admiration at public places, assets developments, avoids mediators for loan and using mobile banking, these variables are not considered for significant development due to negative value of mean difference.

The mean score of the development variable 'Planning' is 15.18 which is significantly higher than the average level (Mean = 10). It differs by 5.18 (Mean Difference) from the average level. The mean difference lies between the lower limit 4.69 and the upper limit 5.68 with 95% confidence interval of the difference. Planning is the vital criteria for any type of business development. The result shows that the most of the respondents have adequate planning character in their enterprises.

The mean score of the development variable 'Information Seeking' is 14.97 which is significantly higher than the average level (Mean = 10). It differs by 4.97 (Mean Difference) from the average level. The mean difference lies between the lower limit 4.55 and the upper limit 5.59 with 95% confidence interval of the difference. None can succeed in business without gathering information related to the business from the circle of business network. From the result it reveals that most of the respondents practice the skill of 'information Seeking' for the success of their enterprises.

The mean score of the development variable 'Problem Solving' is 14.61 which is significantly higher than the average level (Mean = 10). It differs by 4.61 (Mean Difference) from the average level. The mean difference lies between the lower limit 4.16 and the upper limit 5.05 with 95% confidence interval of the difference. It is a known fact that most of the business stagnates or fails because of many problems which the entrepreneurs fail to solve. But in the study area, most of the respondents are good enough in solving various problems.

The mean score of the development variable 'Confidence' is 14.42 which is significantly higher than the average level (Mean = 10). It differs by 4.42 (Mean Difference) from the average level. The mean difference lies between the lower limit 3.97 and the upper limit 4.87 with 95% confidence interval of the difference. Normally the entrepreneurs face ups and downs in their business. Either over confidence or less confidence leads to their downfall. It is the unprintable law in the world. The right confidence level is the only solution for this problem without any doubt. The confidence of most of the respondents in the study area is good as per the result and it is to be appreciated.

The mean score of the development variable 'Honesty' is 14.58 which is significantly higher than the average level (Mean = 10). It differs by 4.58 (Mean Difference) from the average level. The mean difference lies between the lower limit 4.14 and the upper limit 5.02 with 95% confidence interval of the difference. The soul of any business is honesty. It is concluded that the most of the respondents of the study are in honest in their business dealings.

The mean score of the development variable 'Faithfulness' is 13.97 which is significantly higher than the average level (Mean = 10). It differs by 3.97 (Mean Difference) from the average level. The mean difference lies between the lower limit 3.53 and the upper limit 4.42 with 95% confidence interval of the difference. It is very important for an organization is to build brand loyalty first with the people who work there and then with their customers. In this way the most of the respondents in the study have established the faithfulness in their enterprises.

The mean score of the development variable 'Persuasiveness' is 13.89 which is significantly higher than the average level (Mean = 10). It differs by 3.89 (Mean Difference) from the average level. The mean difference lies between the lower limit 3.44 and the upper limit 4.35 with 95% confidence interval of the difference. Persuasiveness is not just an ability to develop. It is also a strategy to learn. Persuasiveness comes natural for some people, but many people have to work to develop it. Most of the respondents under study have developed it through their vast experience.

The mean score of the development variable 'Positive Environment' is 10.95 which is higher significantly than the average level (Mean = 10). It differs by 0.95 (Mean Difference) from the average level. The mean difference lies between the lower limit 0.41 and the upper limit 1.48 with 95% confidence interval of the difference. Regarding overall business environment, most of the women entrepreneurs are found to be satisfied and they mentioned that, despite traditional negative attitudes, the overall business atmosphere is becoming favorable for women.

The mean score of the development variable 'Social and Family Responsibilities' is 11.59 which is significantly higher than the average level (Mean = 10). It differs by 1.59 (Mean Difference) from the average level. The mean difference lies between the lower limit 1.05 and the upper limit 2.13 with 95% confidence interval of the difference. In the past century, the society and family members were against women to do business. But now most of the respondents mention that the society and family members are very supportive to run and develop their enterprises.

The mean score of the development variable 'Decreasing Social Barriers' is 10.89 which is significantly higher than the average level (Mean = 10). It differs by

0.89 (Mean Difference) from the average level. The mean difference lies between the lower limit 0.35 and the upper limit 1.44 with 95% confidence interval of the difference. Apart from the barriers common to all entrepreneur, women encounter various social barriers. The social barriers discourage the women entrepreneurs in their business so that there is a slack in the development. Most of the respondents reveal that the social barriers against women in enterprises have decreased amazingly.

The mean score of the development variable 'Women Business Network' is 8.92 which is significantly lower than the average level (Mean = 10). It differs negatively by -1.08 (Mean Difference) from the average level. The mean difference lies between the lower limit -1.58 and the upper limit -0.58 with 95% confidence interval of the difference. The result shows that the respondents have to develop relationship with women business network to develop their enterprises.

The mean score of the development variable 'Administrative and Legal Support' is 9.08 which is significantly lower than the average level (Mean = 10). It differs negatively by -0.92 (Mean Difference) from the average level. The mean difference lies between the lower limit -1.39 and the upper limit -0.45 with 95% confidence interval of the difference. Most of the respondents report that they do not get sufficient administrative and legal support from the society for their enterprises development.

The mean score of the development variable 'Admiration at Public Places' is 9.16 which is significantly lower than the average level (Mean = 10). It differs negatively by -0.84 (Mean Difference) from the average level. The mean difference lies between the lower limit -1.36 and the upper limit -0.33 with 95% confidence interval of the difference. The result shows that most of the respondents have not received admiration at public places due to their enterprises.

The mean score of the development variable 'Assets Development' is 8.88 which is significantly lower than the average level (Mean = 10). It differs negatively by -1.12 (Mean Difference) from the average level. The mean difference lies between the lower limit -1.53 and the upper limit -0.70 with 95% confidence interval of the difference. Even though the women entrepreneurs numerically increased, the development in assets due to their enterprises is very poor.

The mean score of the development variable 'Financial Development' is 10.96 which is significantly higher than the average level (Mean = 10). It differs by 0.96 (Mean Difference) from the average level. The mean difference lies between the lower limit 0.46 and the upper limit 1.45 with 95% confidence interval of the difference. The result shows that the financial level of most of the respondents have increased due to their enterprises.

The mean score of the development variable 'Workplace Development' is 11.47 which is significantly higher than the average level (Mean = 10). It differs by 1.47 (Mean Difference) from the average level. The mean difference lies between the lower limit 0.99 and the upper limit 1.95 with 95% confidence interval of the difference. Workplace development is an imperative place for business which should be developed properly, otherwise the business will step down. Most of the respondents remarked that they executed special attention to workplace development by proper administration and by having a proper rapport with the labourers.

The mean score of the development variable 'Environmental Development' is 11.66 which is significantly higher than the average level (Mean = 10). It differs by 1.66 (Mean Difference) from the average level. The mean difference lies between the lower limit 1.19 and the upper limit 2.12 with 95% confidence interval of the difference. It is concluded that the environment is congenial to the respondents due to their attitude, friendly movement and kindness.

The mean score of the development variable 'Marketplace Development' is 11.39 which is significantly higher than the average level (Mean = 10). It differs by 1.39 (Mean Difference) from the average level. The mean difference lies between the lower limit 0.92 and the upper limit 1.87 with 95% confidence interval of the difference. The marketplace is the backbone of the business development. Most of the respondents have stated that maintenance of good relationship in the marketplace has resulted good marketing for their products.

The mean score of the development variable 'Values Development' is 13.24 which is significantly higher than the average level (Mean = 10). It differs by 3.24 (Mean Difference) from the average level. The mean difference lies between the lower limit 2.74 and the upper limit 3.73 with 95% confidence interval of the difference. It is concluded that the values of most of the respondents of the study have increased due to their enterprise.

The mean score of the development variable 'Managerial Skill Development' is 11.76 which is significantly higher than the average level (Mean = 10). It differs by 1.76 (Mean Difference) from the average level. The mean difference lies between the lower limit 1.31 and the upper limit 2.21 with 95% confidence interval of the difference. Most of the respondents under study mentioned that they have developed their managerial skill through experience.

The mean score of the development variable 'Low Margin, More Sales and More Profit' is 10.50 which show insignificant. It differs narrowly by 0.50 (Mean Difference) from the average level. The mean difference lies between the lower limit 0.11 and the upper limit 0.89 with 95% confidence interval of the difference. The result shows that the innovation technique of Low Margin, More Sales and More Profit is not an effortful one for the development of business. The mass of the respondents in the study do not observe the innovational technique of low margin, more sales and more profit for their enterprise development.

The mean score of the development variable 'Best Quality Production' is 13.50 which is significantly higher than the average level (Mean = 10). It differs by 3.50 (Mean Difference) from the average level. The mean difference lies between the lower limit 3.03 and the upper limit 3.97 with 95% confidence interval of the difference. The majority of the respondents noted that the innovational technique of the best quality production is a vital part in their business development. The result proves that they observe this technique in their enterprise development.

The mean score of the development variable 'Effective Communication and Negotiation Skill' is 12.42 which is significantly higher than the average level (Mean = 10). It differs by 2.42 (Mean Difference) from the average level. The mean difference lies between the lower limit 1.93 and the upper limit 2.91 with 95% confidence interval of the difference. An effective communication and negotiation is of prime importance in business deals and development. Business is negotiation. An effective communication is directly proportional to an effective negotiation. The entrepreneurs negotiate to buy, to sell, to conclude contracts with suppliers, to fix the staff salaries and so on. The result reveals that most of the respondents encompass this technique in their enterprise development.

The mean score of the development variable 'Advertisement' is 13.03 which is significantly higher than the average level (Mean = 10). It differs by 3.03 (Mean Difference) from the average level. The mean difference lies between the lower limit 2.60 and the upper limit 3.45 with 95% confidence interval of the difference. Good advertising can promote a continual, healthy growth of a business. Advertisement can be expensive, but without it, an entrepreneur cannot "brand" the enterprise image in the minds of potential clients. Advertisement brands a business in the hearts and minds of customers. Many entrepreneurs resort to advertisement to build a close contact with their clients. Majority of the respondents in the study area spends considerable amount for advertisement for the development of their enterprise.

The mean score of the development variable 'Discount & Prizes' is 10.89 which is significantly higher than the average level (Mean = 10). It differs by 0.89 (Mean Difference) from the average level. The mean difference lies between the lower limit 0.42 and the upper limit 1.37 with 95% confidence interval of the difference. In developing countries such as India, the technique of discount and prizes for a product in business in short term plays a vital role as booster to the development of the business. The result of the study proves that the most of the respondents have supported the innovational technique of discount & prizes for their development of their business.

The mean score of the development variable 'Prompt Delivery & Supply' is 12.89 which is significantly higher than the average level (Mean = 10). It differs by 2.89 (Mean Difference) from the average level. The mean difference lies between the lower limit 2.42 and the upper limit 3.37 with 95% confidence interval of the difference. Delayed delivery of products to the customers earns a bad reputation in the enterprise. This provides an opportunity to the competitors to capture the current customers. So, an ideal entrepreneur takes care of the delivery dates and time and tries to handle the orders promptly and efficiently to keep their customers satisfied and happy. The study proves that majority of the respondents used the innovation technique of Prompt Delivery & Supply in their enterprise.

The mean score of the development variable 'Preparing Action Plan' is 10.74 which is significantly higher than the average level (Mean = 10). It differs by 0.74 (Mean Difference) from the average level. The mean difference lies between the lower limit 0.31 and the upper limit 1.17 with 95% confidence interval of the difference. The preparing action plan is an important intermediate stage. Failing to plan can mean planing to fail. Preparing a satisfactory business plan is a painful but essential exercise. The planning process helps the entrepreneurs to understand clearly what they want to achieve, and how and when they can do it. Even if no external support is needed, a business plan helps to avoid mistakes or recognize hidden opportunities. The result reveals that a bulk of the respondents follows the innovational technique of preparing action plan for their enterprises development.

The mean score of the development variable 'Money Transaction through Bank' is 11.11 which is significantly higher than the average level (Mean = 10). It differs by 1.11 (Mean Difference) from the average level. The mean difference lies between the lower limit 0.79 and the upper limit 1.42 with 95% confidence interval of the difference. The best and the safest way for money transaction is through banks. The result proves that a mass of respondents has made their money transaction through bank for their enterprises.

The mean score of the development variable 'Using Bank Loan Scheme with Subsidy' is 15.89 which is significantly higher than the average level (Mean = 10). It differs by 5.89 (Mean Difference) from the average level. The mean difference lies between the lower limit 5.56 and the upper limit 6.23 with 95% confidence interval of the difference. Almost all public sector banks have special loan schemes for women entrepreneurs. But the bank officials report that low awareness and a passive mindset ensure that there are very few takers. On contrast, the result reveals that many respondents use the bank loan scheme with subsidy for their enterprises development.

The mean score of the development variable 'Direct Approach to the Bank Officials' is 9.50 which is significantly lower than the average level (Mean = 10). It differs negatively by -0.50 (Mean Difference) from the average level. The mean difference lies between the lower limit -0.95 and the upper limit -0.05 with 95% confidence interval of the difference. The women entrepreneurs have to approach the bank officials directly in order to know the loan schemes, procedures and training to develop their business. But the result indicates that a bulk of the respondents under study hesitates to approach the bank officials directly regarding their enterprises.

The mean score of the development variable 'Avoiding the Mediators for Loan' is 9.21 which is significantly lower than the average level (Mean = 10). It differs negatively by -0.79 (Mean Difference) from the average level. The mean difference lies between the lower limit -1.29 and the upper limit -0.29 with 95% confidence interval of the difference. The result reveals that most of the respondents under study have no awareness on banking service and so they approach the mediators. It is a minus point for their enterprises development.

The mean score of the development variable 'Prompt Repayment of the Loan' is 16.95 which is significantly higher than the average level (Mean = 10). It differs by 6.95 (Mean Difference) from the average level. The mean difference lies between the lower limit 6.67 and the upper limit 7.22 with 95% confidence interval of the difference. Prompt repayment of the loan is an honesty policy in enterprises. The result shows that the mass of the respondents is keen in prompt repayment of the bank loan.

The mean score of the development variable 'Regular Contact with Bank Official' is 10.03 which show insignificant difference. It differs narrowly by 0.03 (Mean Difference) from the average level. The mean difference lies between lower limit 0.01 and upper limit 0.05 with 95% confidence interval of the difference. The result proves that the most of the respondents are not in regular touch with the bank officials for the development of their enterprises.

The mean score of the development variable 'Using Mobile Banking' is 8.89 which is significantly lower than the average level (Mean = 10). It differs negatively by -1.11 (Mean Difference) from the average level. The mean difference lies between the lower limit -1.57 and the upper limit -0.65 with 95% confidence interval of the difference. Mobile banking means a financial transaction conducted by logging on to a bank's website using a cell phone, and viewing account balances, making transfers between accounts, or paying bills. It is a term used for performing balance checks, account transactions, payments etc. via a mobile device such as a mobile phone. It is a very useful and time saving process for the women entrepreneurs in order to step up on business development. But the result reveals that the majority of the respondents are not aware of the importance, procedure and usage of mobile banking in their business.

The mean score of the development variable 'Internet Usage' is 10.11 which show insignificant difference. It differs narrowly by 0.11 (Mean Difference) from the average level. The mean difference lies between the lower limit 0.05 and the upper limit 0.15 with 95% confidence interval of the difference. Entrepreneurs may use the internet to increase the success of their business. They can analyze the present status, strategies and various schemes about their business. In this modern world, internet usage is inevitable for the success of a business, but most of the respondents under the study are not having the interest for access internet for their development in enterprises.

The mean score of the development variable 'Prompt Communication' is 13.42 which is significantly higher than the average level (Mean = 10). It differs by 3.42 (Mean Difference) from the average level. The mean difference lies between the lower limit 2.96 and the upper limit 3.88 with 95% confidence interval of the difference. Prompt communication with buyers prevents small problems from growing into big problems. It is the best way to promote good relationship and it ensures satisfaction to the customers, and this is the lifeblood of every successful business. Most of the respondents communicate promptly to their customers and dealers.

The mean score of the development variable 'Accounting & Auditing' is 11.63 which is significantly higher than the average level (Mean = 10). It differs by 1.63 (Mean Difference) from the average level. The mean difference lies between the lower limit 1.16 and the upper limit 2.10 with 95% confidence interval of the difference. Accounting is the backbone of any company. Accounting is an area of assets, liabilities, owner equity, revenue and expenses of an organization. Accounting is often called "the language of business" because it provides much of the information that owners, managers, and investors need to evaluate a company's financial performance. The result reveals that most of the respondents maintain the accounting and auditing system in tact.

The mean score of the development variable 'Budget Preparation' is 9.90 which is significantly lower than the average level (Mean = 10). It differs negatively by -0.10 (Mean Difference) from the average level. The mean difference lies between the lower limit -0.54 and the upper limit -0.35 with 95% confidence interval of the difference. Budget preparation is a common affair in most established companies. Every successful entrepreneur and business owner knows the importance of creating a budget. Not only does it come in handy during tax season, but it paves an easy way to look at the financial state of a company. But most of the respondents of the study do not know the seriousness and importance of budget preparation for their business. It is a serious drawback of the entrepreneurs who do not prepare the budget which is crucial for the development of their enterprises.

The mean score of the development variable 'Examine the Business Network' is 13.68 which is significantly higher than the average level (Mean = 10). It differs by 3.68 (Mean Difference) from the average level. The mean difference lies between the lower limit 3.22 and the upper limit 4.15 with 95% confidence interval of the difference. Examining the business network is one of the most important intellectual parts of a successful entrepreneur. Good entrepreneurs examine the business around them regularly in order to develop their business. The result shows that most of the respondents do examine the business network around their enterprises.

The mean score of the development variable 'Computerized Work' is 10.50 which show insignificant difference. It differs narrowly by 0.50 (Mean Difference) from the average level. The mean difference lies between the lower limit 0.02 and the upper limit 0.98 with 95% confidence interval of the difference. It is difficult to think of a situation where businesses can be done without electronic technology or computers today. Certain powerful, yet simple software has come to the rescue of small businesses in reducing their tasks and opening up new channels. Simple applications like spreadsheets and word processing help them maintain accounts, finances and keep track of correspondence. These applications allow the users to customize reports and other functions to suit their particular business. But the result shows that the computerized work in enterprises among the respondents is very less.

5.2 One-Sample t Test of the Categories of Women Entrepreneurs in Various Development

HYPOTHESIS II

Null Hypothesis: There is no significant Personality Development in all categories of women entrepreneurs.

Table 5.2

One-Sample t Test of the Categories of Women Entrepreneurs - Personality Development

Categories of Women Entrepreneurs	Test Value = 10						
	Mean	SD	t value	P value	Mean Diff.	95% Confidence Interval of the Diff.	
						Lower	Upper
Women Managed Unit	14.80	4.47	43.87	.000**	4.80	4.58	5.02
Jointly Managed Unit	14.09	4.45	24.92	.000**	4.09	3.77	4.42
Men Managed Unit	13.89	4.47	14.22	.000**	3.89	3.36	4.43

**Significant at .05 level of confidence

Since P value is less than 0.05, the null hypothesis is rejected at 5% level of significance with regard to mean of all categories of women entrepreneurs in Personality Development. Hence there is a significant development of Personality development in all categories of women entrepreneurs.

The mean score of the categories of women entrepreneurs of the 'Women Managed Unit' is 14.80 which is significantly higher than the average level (Mean = 10). It differs by 4.80 (Mean Difference) from the average level.

The mean score of the categories of women entrepreneurs of the 'Jointly Managed Unit' is 14.09 which is significantly higher than the average level (Mean = 10). It differs by 4.09 (Mean Difference) from the average level.

The mean score of the categories of women entrepreneurs of the 'Men Managed Unit' is 13.89 which is significantly higher than the average level (Mean = 10). It differs by 3.89 (Mean Difference) from the average level.

HYPOTHESIS III

Null Hypothesis: There is no significant Social Development in all categories of women entrepreneurs.

Table 5.3

One-Sample t Test of the Categories of Women Entrepreneurs - Social Development

Categories of Women Entrepreneurs	Test Value = 10						
	Mean	SD	t value	P value	Mean Diff.	95% Confidence Interval of the Diff.	
						Lower	Upper
Women Managed Unit	10.74	5.34	5.26	.000**	0.74	0.47	1.02
Jointly Managed Unit	8.97	4.80	-5.37	.000**	-1.03	-1.41	-0.66
Men Managed Unit	9.16	5.12	-2.48	.014**	-0.84	-1.51	-0.17

**Significant at .05 level of confidence

Since P value is less than 0.05, the null hypothesis is rejected at 5% level of significance with regard to mean of the category of women managed unit of women entrepreneurs in Social Development. Hence there is a significant development of Social Development in women managed unit of women entrepreneurs.

The mean score of the categories of women entrepreneurs of the 'Women Managed Unit' is 10.74 which is significantly higher than the average level (Mean = 10). It differs by 0.74 (Mean Difference) from the average level.

Since the mean difference are negative value, the null hypothesis is failed to reject even though the P value is less than 0.05 at 5% level of significance with regard to mean of the category of jointly managed unit and men managed unit of women entrepreneurs in Social Development. Hence there is no significant development in Social Development in jointly managed unit and men managed unit of women entrepreneurs.

HYPOTHESIS IV

Null Hypothesis: There is no significant Personal Development in all categories of women entrepreneurs.

Table 5.4

One-Sample t Test of the Categories of Women Entrepreneurs - Personal Development

Categories of Women Entrepreneurs	Test Value = 10						
	Mean	SD	t value	P value	Mean Diff.	95% Confidence Interval of the Diff.	
						Lower	Upper
Women Managed Unit	10.82	4.73	7.12	.000**	0.82	0.60	1.05
Jointly Managed Unit	12.36	4.89	13.01	.000**	2.36	2.00	2.71
Men Managed Unit	11.76	4.47	6.42	.000**	1.76	1.22	2.30

**Significant at .05 level of confidence

Since P value is less than 0.05, the null hypothesis is rejected at 5% level of significance with regard to mean of all categories of women entrepreneurs in Personal Development. Hence there is a significant development in Personal Development in all categories of women entrepreneurs.

The mean score of the categories of women entrepreneurs of the 'Women Managed Unit' is 10.82 which is significantly higher than the average level (Mean = 10). It differs by 0.82 (Mean Difference) from the average level.

The mean score of the categories of women entrepreneurs of the 'Jointly Managed Unit' is 12.36 which is significantly higher than the average level (Mean = 10). It differs by 2.36 (Mean Difference) from the average level.

The mean score of the categories of women entrepreneurs of the 'Men Managed Unit' is 11.76 which is significantly higher than the average level (Mean = 10). It differs by 1.76 (Mean Difference) from the average level.

HYPOTHESIS V

Null Hypothesis: There is no significant Innovational Development in all categories of women entrepreneurs.

Table 5.5

One-Sample t Test of the Categories of Women Entrepreneurs - Innovational Development

Categories of Women Entrepreneurs	Test Value = 10						
	Mean	SD	t value	P value	Mean Diff.	95% Confidence Interval of the Diff.	
						Lower	Upper
Women Managed Unit	12.25	4.83	19.06	.000**	2.25	2.02	2.49
Jointly Managed Unit	11.87	4.77	10.55	.000**	1.87	1.52	2.21
Men Managed Unit	10.74	4.26	2.82	.005**	0.74	0.22	1.25

**Significant at .05 level of confidence

Since P value is less than 0.05, the null hypothesis is rejected at 5% level of significance with regard to mean of all categories of women managed unit in

Innovational development. Hence there is a significant development in Innovational Development in all categories of women entrepreneurs.

The mean score of the categories of women entrepreneurs of the 'Women Managed Unit' is 12.25 which is significantly higher than the average level (Mean = 10). It differs by 2.25 (Mean Difference) from the average level.

The mean score of the categories of women entrepreneurs of the 'Jointly Managed Unit' is 11.87 which is significantly higher than the average level (Mean = 10). It differs by 1.87 (Mean Difference) from the average level.

The mean score of the categories of women entrepreneurs of the 'Men Managed Unit' is 10.74 which is significantly higher than the average level (Mean = 10). It differs by 0.74 (Mean Difference) from the average level.

HYPOTHESIS VI

Null Hypothesis: There is no significant Embankment Development in all categories of women entrepreneurs.

Table 5.6

One-Sample t Test of the Categories of Women Entrepreneurs - Embankment Development

Categories of Women Entrepreneurs	Test Value = 10						
	Mean	SD	t value	P value	Mean Diff.	95% Confidence Interval of the Diff.	
						Lower	Upper
Women Managed Unit	11.93	4.95	15.87	.000**	1.93	1.69	2.16
Jointly Managed Unit	12.04	5.06	10.89	.000**	2.04	1.67	2.41
Men Managed Unit	8.89	4.56	-3.95	.000**	-1.11	-1.66	-0.55

**Significant at .05 level of confidence

Since P value is less than 0.05, the null hypothesis is rejected at 5% level of significance with regard to mean of women managed unit and jointly managed unit of women entrepreneurs in Embankment Development. Hence there is a significant development in Embankment Development in women managed units and jointly managed unit of women entrepreneurs.

The mean score of the categories of women entrepreneurs of the 'Women Managed Unit' is 11.93 which is significantly higher than the average level (Mean = 10). It differs by 1.93 (Mean Difference) from the average level.

The mean score of the categories of women entrepreneurs of the 'Jointly Managed Unit' is 12.04 which is significantly higher than the average level (Mean = 10). It differs by 2.04 (Mean Difference) from the average level.

Since the mean difference is negative value, the null hypothesis is failed to reject even as the P value is less than 0.05 at 5% level of significance with regard to mean of the category of men managed unit of women entrepreneurs in Embankment Development. Hence there is no significant development in Embankment Development in men managed unit of women entrepreneurs.

HYPOTHESIS VII

Null Hypothesis: There is no significant Intellectual Development in all categories of women entrepreneurs.

Table 5.7

One-Sample t Test of the Categories of Women Entrepreneurs -

Intellectual Development

Categories of Women Entrepreneurs	Test Value = 10						
	Mean	SD	t value	P value	Mean Diff.	95% Confidence Interval of the Diff.	
						Lower	Upper
Women Managed Unit	11.38	4.65	11.22	.000**	1.38	1.14	1.62
Jointly Managed Unit	12.29	4.97	11.49	.000**	2.29	1.90	2.68
Men Managed Unit	10.50	4.78	1.58	.056	0.50	-0.12	1.12

**Significant at .05 level of confidence

Since P value is less than 0.05, the null hypothesis is rejected at 5% level of significance with regard to mean of women managed and jointly managed unit of women entrepreneurs in Intellectual development. Hence there is a significant development in Intellectual development in women managed and jointly managed units of women entrepreneurs.

The mean score of the categories of women entrepreneurs of the 'Women Managed Unit' is 11.38 which is significantly higher than the average level (Mean = 10). It differs by 1.38 (Mean Difference) from the average level.

The mean score of the categories of women entrepreneurs of the 'Jointly Managed Unit' is 12.29 which is significantly higher than the average level (Mean = 10). It differs by 2.29 (Mean Difference) from the average level.

Since P value is more than 0.05, the null hypothesis is failed to reject at 5% level of significance with regard to mean of the category of men managed unit of women entrepreneurs in Intellectual Development. Hence there is no significant development in Intellectual Development in Men managed unit of women entrepreneurs.

5.3 Factor Analysis of the Development Factors of Women Entrepreneurs

The various development factors of women entrepreneurs namely personality development, social development, personal development, innovational development, embankment development and intellectual development were analyzed with the help of Factor Analysis.

Factor analysis attempts to identify underlying variables or factors that explain the pattern of correlations within a set of observed variables. Factor analysis is often used in data reduction to identify a small number of factors that explain most of the variance observed in a much larger number of manifest variables. It is a technique which analyses correlations between variables. There are two stages in Factor analysis. Stage I is the Factor Extraction process. The most popular method is called Principal Component Analysis (PCA), based on the computation of an Eigen value. It translates approximately the 'variance explained' concept of regression analysis. The higher the Eigen value of a factor, the higher is the amount of variance explained by the factor. As the objective is to reduce the variables to a fewer number of Factors, those with Eigen value of 1 or more are retained.

The stage II is rotation of Principal Components. After the number of extracted Factors is decided upon in stage I, the next task is to interpret and name the factors. Here the Factor matrix is used for the purpose of identifying the factors which are associated with the original variables. The Factor matrix gives the loading of each variable on each of the extracted factors. This is similar to a correlation matrix, with 'loadings' which have values between 0 and 1. Values close to 1 represent high loadings and those close to 0, low loadings. The objective is to find variables which have a high loading on one factor, but low loadings on the other factors.

Table 5.8

KMO and Bartlett's Test of Sampling Adequacy

Kaiser-Meyer-Olkin Measure of Sampling Adequacy		.853
Bartlett's Test of Sphericity	Approx. Chi-Square	9115.117
	df	15
	Sig.	.000**

**Significant at .05 level of confidence

The Kaiser-Meyer-Olkin statistic varies between 0 and 1. A value of 0 indicates that the sum of partial correlations is large relative to the sum of correlations, indicating diffusion in the pattern of correlations (hence, Factor analysis is likely to be inappropriate). A value close to 1 indicates that patterns of correlations are relatively compact and so factor analysis should yield distinct and reliable factors. Furthermore, values between 0.5 and 0.7 are mediocre, values between 0.7 and 0.8 are good, values between 0.8 and 0.9 are great and values above 0.9 are superb. For these data the value is 0.853, which falls into the range of being great. So, one should be confident that factor analysis is appropriate for these data.

For Factor analysis to work some relationships between variables are needed and if the R-matrix is an identity matrix then all correlation coefficients will be zero. Therefore, this test is to be significant. A significant test reveals that the R-matrix is not an identity matrix; there are some relationships between the variables. Bartlett's test is highly significant ($p < 0.001$), and therefore factor analysis is appropriate.

Table 5.9

Factors Analysis for the Development Factors of Women Entrepreneurs

Development Factors	Eigen value	Variance %	Cumulative %
Personality Development	95.478	67.383	67.383
Social Development	14.431	10.184	77.568
Personal Development	12.221	8.625	86.193
Innovational Development	9.642	6.805	92.998
Embankment Development	5.749	4.057	97.055
Intellectual Development	4.173	2.945	100.00

For the Eigen values over option the default is Kaiser's recommendation of Eigen values over 1. There are six factors with Eigen value more than 1. The table 5.9 lists the Eigen values associated with each linear component (factor). The above table shows each factor, its Eigen value, variance percentage and its cumulative percentage. The Eigen values associated with each factor represent the variance explained by that particular linear component. The table also displays the Eigen value in terms of the percentage of variance explained. It shows clearly that the first three factors explain relatively large amounts of variance whereas subsequent factors explain only small amounts of variance. It is observed from the cumulative percentage column that six factors extracted together account for 100 per cent of the total variance.

Table 5.10

Factor Analysis of loading for the Variables of Development Factors

Factors	Variables	Loading
Personality Development	Planning	0.958
	Information Seeking	0.874
	Problem Solving	0.865
	Confidence	0.852
	Honesty	0.874
	Faithfulness	0.745
	Persuasiveness	0.807
Social Development	Positive Environment	0.887
	Family and Social Responsibilities	0.634
	Decreasing Social Barriers	0.906
	Women Business Network	0.908
	Administrative and Legal Support	0.855
	Admiration at Public Places	0.865
Personal Development	Assets Development	0.681
	Financial Development	0.710
	Workplace Development	0.892
	Environmental Development	0.846
	Marketplace Development	0.895
	Values Development	0.903
	Managerial Skill Development	0.857
Innovational Development	Low Margin, More Sales & More Profit	0.915
	Best Quality Production	0.903
	Effective Communication & Negotiation Skills	0.825
	Advertisement	0.822
	Discount & Prizes	0.895
	Prompt Delivery & Supply	0.892
	Preparing Action Plan	0.839
Embankment	Money Transaction through Bank	0.737
	Using Bank Loan Schemes with Subsidy	0.785

Development	Direct Approach to the Bank Officials	0.843
	Avoiding the Mediators for Loan	0.924
	Prompt Repayment of the Loan Amount	0.763
	Regular Contact with Bank Officials	0.846
	Using Mobile Banking	0.864
Intellectual Development	Internet Usage	0.805
	Prompt Communication	0.775
	Accounting & Auditing	0.890
	Budget Preparation	0.595
	Examining the Business Network	0.897
	Computerized Work	0.879

The first Factor consists of seven variables namely, planning, information seeking, problem solving, confidence, honesty, faithfulness and persuasiveness. These variables have loadings of 0.958, 0.874, 0.865, 0.852, 0.874, 0.745 and 0.807 respectively. These variables have high loadings on Factor I. The Factor I can be called 'Personality Development' to capture the essence of these seven variables. The Factor I explain 67.383 per cent of the total variance and the Eigen value is 95.478 as shown in table 5.9.

The second Factor comprises of six variables namely, positive environment, family and social responsibilities, decreasing social barriers, women business network, administrative and legal support and admiration at public places. These variables have loadings of 0.887, 0.634, 0.906, 0.908, 0.855 and 0.865 respectively. These variables have high loadings on Factor II which can be called 'Social Development' to represent the theme of these seven variables. It explains 10.184 per cent of the total variance and the Eigen value is 14.431 as shown in table 5.9.

The third Factor comprises of seven variables namely, assets development, financial development, workplace development, environmental development, marketplace development, values development and managerial skill development. These variables have high loadings on Factor III which can be called 'Personal Development' to represent the theme of these seven variables. These variables have loadings of 0.681, 0.710, 0.892, 0.846, 0.895, 0.903 and 0.857 respectively. Its Eigen value is 12.221 and it explains 8.625 per cent of the total variance as shown in table 5.9.

The fourth Factor consists of seven variables namely, low margin, more sales & more profit, best quality production, effective communication & negotiation skills, advertisement, discount & prizes, prompt delivery & supply and preparing action plan. These variables have high loadings on Factor IV which can be called 'Innovational Development' to represent the theme of these seven variables. These variables have loadings of 0.915, 0.903, 0.825, 0.822, 0.895, 0.892 and 0.839 respectively. Its Eigen value is 9.642 and it explains 6.805 per cent of the total variance as shown in table 5.9.

The fifth Factor consists of seven variables namely, money transaction through bank, using bank loan, direct approach to the bank officials, avoiding the mediators for loan, prompt repayment of the loan amount, regular contact with bank officials and using mobile banking. These variables have loadings of 0.737, 0.785, 0.843, 0.924, 0.763, 0.846 and 0.864 respectively. These variables have high loadings on Factor V which can be called 'Embankment Development' to represent the theme of these seven variables. Its Eigen value is 5.749 and it explains 4.057 per cent of the total variance as shown in table 5.9.

The sixth Factor consists of six variables namely, internet usage, prompt communication, accounting & auditing, budget preparation, examines the business network and computerized work. These variables have high loadings on Factor VI which can be called 'Intellectual Development' to represent the theme of these seven variables. These variables have loadings of 0.805, 0.775, 0.890, 0.595, 0.897 and 0.879 respectively. Its Eigen value is 4.173 and it explains 2.945 per cent of the total variance as shown in table 5.9.

Table 5.11

Factors Analysis of Loadings for the Development Factors

S.No	Factors	Loading
1	Personality Development	0.561
2	Social Development	0.768
3	Personal Development	0.860
4	Innovational Development	0.895
5	Embankment Development	0.771
6	Intellectual Development	0.866

The development Factor consists of six factors namely, personality development, social development, personal development, innovational development, embankment development and intellectual development. These Factors have loadings of 0.561, 0.768, 0.860, 0.895, 0.771 and 0.866 respectively. Its Eigen values are 95.478, 14.431, 12.221, 9.642, 5.749 and 4.173 respectively and it explains 67.383, 10.184, 8.625, 6.805, 4.057 and 2.945 per cent of the total variance respectively as shown in table 5.9.

Table 5.12

Correlation Matrix of the Development Factors

	Personality	Social	Personal	Innovational	Embankment	Intellectual
Personality	1.000	.471	.535	.546	.425	.426
Social	.471	1.000	.645	.695	.539	.670
Personal	.535	.645	1.000	.814	.535	.670
Innovational	.546	.695	.814	1.000	.567	.718
Embankment	.425	.539	.535	.567	1.000	.695
Intellectual	.426	.670	.670	.718	.695	1.000
Personality		.000	.000	.000	.000	.000
Social	.000		.000	.000	.000	.000
Personal	.000	.000		.000	.000	.000
Innovational	.000	.000	.000		.000	.000
Embankment	.000	.000	.000	.000		.000
Intellectual	.000	.000	.000	.000	.000	

There is a significant relationship between various development factors of women entrepreneurs as shown in the above table. It is proved at 5% level of significance. Around 55 per cent of Innovational Development is related to the Personality Development of women entrepreneurs. Similarly, 54 per cent of the Personal Development is related to the Personality Development of women entrepreneurs. On the other hand, Innovational Development helps the Social Development for about 70 per cent. Similarly 67 per cent of Intellectual Development is related to the Social Development of women entrepreneurs.

Innovational Development helps the Personal Development for about 81 per cent. Also 67 per cent of Intellectual Development is related to the Personal

Development of women entrepreneurs. The Intellectual Development supports them to develop the Innovational arena for about 72 per cent and 70 per cent of Intellectual Development supports them to develop the Embankment Development as shown in the above table.

It is very evident from the above table that there is a significant relationship between the factors of various developments of women entrepreneurs. It also indicates the necessity of the application of the statistical tool. Otherwise, it might be concluded that the various developments are independent and mutually exclusive to each other. The above correlation coefficient table proves that the various developments are highly correlated, inter linked and inter dependent.

5.4 Friedman Test of the Variables of Development Factor

Friedman Test of Non Parametric statistics was used to find out the significant difference between the variables of development factors of women entrepreneurs. The test statistic for the Friedman's test is a Chi-square with a-1 degrees of freedom, where 'a' is the number of repeated measures. When the P-value for this test is small (usually <0.05) there is an evidence to reject the null hypothesis. If the Friedman Test result was statistically significant then Wilcoxon Signed-Rank Tests was used as post-hoc test to examine where the differences actually occur. The new significance level of Bonferroni adjustment was calculated by divide the actual significance level (0.05) by the number of tests was running. As the main focus is usually on the development factors not on its variables, it is sufficient to discuss the development factors effect only. Hence, the development factors effect only is discussed.

HYPOTHESIS VIII

Null Hypothesis: There is no significant difference among Mean Rank of variables of Factor – Personality Development.

Table 5.13

Friedman Test of the Variables of Personality Development Factor

Variables	Mean Rank	Chi-square Value	P Value
Planning	4.89		
Information Seeking	4.38		
Problem Solving	4.13		
Confidence	4.04	170.093	0.000**
Honesty	3.99		
Faithfulness	3.28		
Persuasiveness	3.30		

**Significant at .05 level of confidence

Since P value is less than 0.05, the null hypothesis is rejected at 5% level of significance with regard to the mean rank of the variables of factor - Personality Development of women entrepreneurs. At the α = 0.05 level of significance, there exists enough evidence to conclude that there is a significant difference among the true means of seven variables of Personality Development in women entrepreneurs.

The mean rank of the 'Planning' is 4.89 which is the most dominant variable under Personality Development. The second most important variable based on the mean rank is 'Information Seeking' and its rank is 4.38 and the least variable is 'Faithfulness' and its rank is 3.28 as shown above in the table 5.13. The extent of impact of each variable of Factor – Personality Development can be seen from the mean rank. If the mean rank is higher, there is a great development and if the mean rank is lower, there is a slight development.

HYPOTHESIS IX

Null Hypothesis: There is no significant difference among Mean Rank of variables of Factor – Social Development.

Table 5.14

Friedman Test of the Variables of Social Development Factor

Variables	Mean Rank	Chi-square Value	P Value
Positive Environment	4.21		
Social & Family Responsibilities	3.76		
Decreasing Social Barriers	4.21	270.586	0.000**
Women Business Network	2.73		
Administrative and Legal Support	2.97		
Admiration at Public Places	3.13		

**Significant at .05 level of confidence

Since P value is less than 0.05, the null hypothesis is rejected at 5% level of significance with regard to the mean rank of the variables of Factor - Social Development of women entrepreneurs. At the α = 0.05 level of significance, there exists enough evidence to conclude that there is a significant difference among the true means of seven variables of Social Development in women entrepreneurs.

The mean rank of the 'Positive Environment' and 'Decreasing Social Barriers' are 4.21 which are equally most dominant variables under Social Development. The second most important variable based on the mean rank is 'Social and Family Responsibilities' and its rank is 3.76 and the least variable is 'Women Business Network' and its rank is 2.73 as shown above in the table 5.14. If the mean rank is higher, there is a great development and if the mean rank is lower, there is a slight development.

HYPOTHESIS X

Null Hypothesis: There is no significant difference among Mean Rank of variables of Factor – Personal Development.

Table 5.15

Friedman Test of the Variables of Personal Development Factor

Variables	Mean Rank	Chi-square Value	P Value
Assets Development	2.16		
Financial Development	3.80		
Workplace Development	4.05		
Environmental Development	4.43	510.307	0.000**
Marketplace Development	4.13		
Values Development	5.30		
Managerial Skill Development	4.13		

**Significant at .05 level of confidence

Since P value is less than 0.05, the null hypothesis is rejected at 5% level of significance with regard to the mean rank of the variables of Factor "Personal Development" of women entrepreneurs. At the $\alpha = 0.05$ level of significance, there exists enough evidence to conclude that there is a significant difference among the means of seven variables of Personal Development in women entrepreneurs.

The mean rank of the 'Values Development' is 5.30 which is the most dominant variables under Personal Development. The second most important variable based on the mean rank is 'Environmental Development' and its rank is 4.43 and the least variable is 'Assets Development' and its rank is 2.16 as shown above in the table 5.15. If the mean rank is higher, there is a great development and if the mean rank is lower, there is a slight development.

HYPOTHESIS XI

Null Hypothesis: There is no significant difference among Mean Rank of variables of Factor – Innovational Development.

Table 5.16

Friedman Test of the Variables of Innovational Development Factor

Variables	Mean Rank	Chi-square Value	P Value
Low Margin, More Sales & More Profit	2.75		
Best Quality Production	5.22		
Effective Communication & Negotiation	4.30		
Advertisement	4.91	524.100	0.000**
Discount & Prizes	3.20		
Prompt Delivery & Supply	4.55		
Preparing Action Plan	3.07		

**Significant at .05 level of confidence

Since P value is less than 0.05, the null hypothesis is rejected at 5% level of significance with regard to the mean rank of variable of Factor - Innovational Development of women entrepreneurs. At the $\alpha = 0.05$ level of significance, there exists enough evidence to conclude that there is a significant difference among the true mean of seven variables of Innovational Development in women entrepreneurs.

The mean rank of the 'Best Quality Production' is 5.22 which is the most dominant variable under Innovational Development. The second most important variable based on the mean rank is 'Advertisement' and its rank is 4.91 and the least variable is 'Low Margin, More Sales & More Profit' and its rank is 2.75 as shown above in the table 5.16. If the mean rank is higher, there is a great development and if the mean rank is lower, there is a slight development.

HYPOTHESIS XII

Null Hypothesis: There is no significant difference among Mean Rank of variables of Factor – Embankment Development.

Table 5.17

Friedman Test of the Variables of Embankment Development Factor

Variables	Mean Rank	Chi-square Value	P Value
Money Transaction through Bank	4.01		
Using Bank Loan Schemes with Subsidy	6.16		
Direct Approach to the Bank Officials	3.05		
Avoiding Mediators for Loan	2.66	1339.208	0.000**
Prompt Repayment of the Loan Amount	6.32		
Regular Contact with Bank Officials	3.39		
Using Mobile Banking	2.41		

**Significant at .05 level of confidence

Since P value is less than 0.05, the null hypothesis is rejected at 5% level of significance with regard to the mean rank of variables of Factor - Embankment Development of women entrepreneurs. At the $\alpha = 0.05$ level of significance, there exists enough evidence to conclude that there is a significant difference in the true mean of seven variables of Embankment Development in women entrepreneurs.

The mean rank of the 'Prompt Repayment of the Loan Amount' is 6.32 which is the most dominant variable under Embankment Development. The second most important variable based on the mean rank is 'Using Bank Loan Scheme with Subsidy' and its rank is 6.16 and the least variable is 'Using Mobile Banking' and its rank is 2.41 as shown above in the table 5.17. If the mean rank is higher, there is a great development and if the mean rank is lower, there is a slight development.

HYPOTHESIS XIII

Null Hypothesis: There is no significant difference among Mean Rank of variables of Factor – Intellectual Development.

Table 5.18

Friedman Test of the Variables of Intellectual Development Factor

Variables	Mean Rank	Chi-square Value	P Value
Internet Usage	2.83		
Prompt Communication	4.81		
Accounting & Auditing	3.64	779.534	0.000**
Budget Preparation	2.16		
Examining the Business Network	4.83		
Computerized Work	2.74		

**Significant at .05 level of confidence

Since P value is less than 0.05, the null hypothesis is rejected at 5% level of significance with regard to the mean rank of variables of Factor -Intellectual Development of women entrepreneurs. At the $\alpha = 0.05$ level of significance, there exists enough evidence to conclude that there is a significant difference in the mean of seven variables of Intellectual Development in women entrepreneurs.

The mean rank of the 'Examining the Business Network' is 4.83 which is the most dominant variable under Intellectual Development. The second most important variable based on the mean rank is 'Prompt Communication' and its rank is 4.81 and the least variable is 'Budget Preparation' its rank is 2.16 as shown above in the table 5.18. If the mean rank is higher, there is a great development and if the mean rank is lower, there is a slight development.

HYPOTHESIS XIV

Null Hypothesis: There is no significant difference among the Mean Rank of Development Factors of Women Entrepreneurs

Table 5.19

Friedman Test of the Development Factors

Development Factors	Mean Rank	Chi-square Value	P Value
Personality Development	4.89		
Social Development	2.50		
Personal Development	3.19	2244.812	0.000**
Innovational Development	3.69		
Embankment Development	3.49		
Intellectual Development	3.24		

**Significant at .05 level of confidence

Since P value is less than 0.05, the null hypothesis is rejected at 5% level of significance with regard to the mean rank of the Development Factors of women entrepreneurs. At the $\alpha = 0.05$ level of significance, there exists enough evidence to conclude that there is a significant difference in the mean of six Development Factors in women entrepreneurs.

The mean rank of the factor 'Personality Development' is 4.89 which is the most dominant factor under of the Development Factors. The second most important factor based on the mean rank is 'Innovational Development' and its rank is 3.69 and the least factor is 'Social Development' and its rank is 2.50 as shown above in the table 5.19. If the mean rank is higher, there is greater development and if the mean rank is lower, there is slightest development.

The Chi-square value (2244.812) for the development factors is significant at 0.05 level of confidence. It means that there is a significant difference among the means of the factors. Hence Wilcoxon Signed-Rank Test has been applied as the post-hoc test to examine where the differences actually occur. The new significance level of Bonferroni adjustment was calculated by divide the actual significance level (0.05) by the number of tests were running (0.05/15 = 0.003). Post-hoc analysis with Wilcoxon

Signed-Rank Tests was conducted with a Bonferroni correction applied, resulting in a significance level set at P < 0.003. This means that if the P value is larger than 0.003 then there was no statistically significant result. The results of Wilcoxon Signed-Rank Test for the development factors have been presented in Table 5.20.

Table 5.20

Wilcoxon Signed-Rank Test of the Development Factors

Development Factors	Z Value	P Value
Personality Development and Social Development	-34.945	.000**
Personality Development and Personal Development	-29.679	.000**
Personality Development and Innovational Development	-26.072	.000**
Personality Development and Embankment Development	-24.433	.000**
Personality Development and Intellectual Development	-28.560	.000**
Social Development and Personal Development	-16.985	.000**
Social Development and Innovational Development	-23.460	.000**
Social Development and Embankment Development	-14.737	.000**
Social Development and Intellectual Development	-16.275	.000**
Personal Development and Innovational Development	-10.455	.000**
Personal Development and Embankment Development	-1.815	.070
Personal Development and Intellectual Development	-1.364	.173
Innovational Development and Embankment Development	-4.847	.000**
Innovational Development and Intellectual Development	-10.324	.000**
Embankment Development and Intellectual Development	-5.375	.000**

**Significant at .05 level of confidence

The table 5.20 shows the output of the Wilcoxon Signed-Rank Test on each of the combinations. There are no significant differences between the Personal

Development and Embankment Development (Z = -1.815, P = 0.070) and between Personal Development and Intellectual Development (Z = -1.364, P = 0.173). However, there was a statistically significant difference between Personality Development and Social Development (Z = -34.945, P = 0.000), Personality Development and Personal Development (Z = -29.679, P = 0.000), Personality Development and Innovational Development (Z = -26.072, P = 0.000), Personality Development and Embankment Development (Z = -24.433, P = 0.000), Personality Development and Intellectual Development (Z = -28.560, P = 0.000), Social Development and Personal Development (Z = -16.985, P = 0.000), Social Development and Innovational Development (Z = -23.460, P = 0.000), Social Development and Embankment Development (Z = -14.747, P = 0.000), Social Development and Intellectual Development (Z = -16.275, P = 0.000), Personal Development and Innovational Development (Z = -10.455, P = 0.000), Innovational Development and Embankment Development (Z = -4.847, P = 0.000), Innovational Development and Intellectual Development (Z = -10.324, P = 0.000) and Embankment Development and Intellectual Development (Z = -5.375, P = 0.000).

Table 5.21

Mean and Standard Deviation of the Development Factors

Factors	Mean	SD
Personality Development	14.518	4.478
Social Development	10.098	5.241
Personal Development	11.338	4.795
Innovational Development	11.996	4.780
Embankment Development	11.654	5.028
Intellectual Development	11.541	4.782

The mean of Personality Development is 14.518 which show that it is the most dominant factors among the factors of various developments of women entrepreneurs. The other important factor which is gained and experienced by the women entrepreneurs is Innovational Development which mean is 11.996 followed by the factor Embankment Development which mean is 11.654. It cannot be concluded that Personality and Innovational Developments would be the dominant ones for ever. Perhaps, the time frame required for these developments could be shorter and also the most essential ones. And also the other factors would have been equally dominated with these factors when the women entrepreneurs get more experience in their business. Furthermore, as the women entrepreneurs gain more experience, the important factors would change and their extent of development would also change over a period of time. It can be inferred that the significant development felt by many of the women entrepreneurs are Personality and Innovational Developments.

The extent of development of each variable can be seen from the mean rank. Here, the variables are development factors of women entrepreneurs. The higher the mean, the greater is the development and the lower the mean, the less is the development.

CHAPTER VI

ANALYSIS AND INTERPREATIONS OF THE CONSTRAINTS AND PERCEPTION ON BANKING SERVICE

This chapter deals with the analysis and interpretations of various constraints of the respondents and their Perception on Banking Service in Tirunelveli district. The Factor analysis of the various constraints of women entrepreneurs is done in the first part and GAP analysis of the perception of women entrepreneurs on Banking Service is done in the second part of the chapter.

6.1   Factor Analysis of the Constraints of Women Entrepreneurs

There are various barriers to women entrepreneurs in running their business in Tirunelveli District. It is a known fact that personal characteristics and social aspects are major factors in developing entrepreneurship. The study analyzes the most important women centred constraints after carefully referring the journals and books and after having serious discussions with experienced women entrepreneurs. Multiple roles of the women entrepreneurs, marketing competitions with males, gender discriminations, negative attitudes of the society, health problems, social barriers, unsecured communication system, sexual harassment, family restriction and religious beliefs & traditional customs are the constraints faced by the women entrepreneurs.

Table 6.1

Factor Analysis of the Constraints

Factor	Variables	Loading
Constraints of Women Entrepreneurs	Multiple Roles of the Women Entrepreneurs	0.851
	Marketing Competitions with Males	0.466
	Gender Discriminations	0.929
	Negative Attitudes of the Society	0.272
	Health Problems	0.930
	Social Barriers	0.924
	Insecure Communication System	0.924
	Sexual Harassment	0.905
	Family Restriction	0.906
	Religious Beliefs and Traditional Customs	0.918

The factor of constraints of women entrepreneurs consists of ten variables namely, Multiple Roles of the Women Entrepreneurs, Marketing competitions with Males, Gender Discriminations, Negative Attitudes of Society, Health Problems, Social Barriers, Insecure Communication System, Sexual Harassment, Family Restriction and Religious Beliefs & Traditional Customs. These variables have loadings of 0.851, 0.466, 0.929, 0.272, 0.930, 0.924, 0.924, 0.905, 0.906 and 0.918 respectively. These variables have high loadings on factor of constraints except Negative Attitudes of the Society and marketing competitions with Males.

HYPOTHESIS XV

Null Hypothesis: There is no significant difference among Mean Rank variables of Constraints of Women Entrepreneurs.

Table 6.2

Friedman Test of the Constraints

Constraints of Women Entrepreneurs	Mean Rank	Chi-square Value	P Value
Multiple Roles of the Women Entrepreneurs	6.35		
Marketing Competitions with Males	7.04		
Gender Discriminations	5.20		
Negative Attitudes of the Society	5.80		
Health Problems	7.11	1093.975	0.000**
Social Barriers	7.12		
Insecure Communication System	3.31		
Sexual Harassment	6.38		
Family Restriction	3.37		
Religious Beliefs and Traditional Customs	3.32		

**Significant at .05 level of confidence

Since P value is less than 0.05, the null hypothesis is rejected at 5% level of significance with regard to the mean rank of the variables of the constraints of women entrepreneurs. Hence there is a significant difference among the variables of the constraints of women entrepreneurs.

The mean rank of constraint 'Social Barriers' is 7.12 which is the most dominant variables under Constraints Factor of women entrepreneurs. The second most important mean rank is 'Health Problems' which is 7.11 and the least variables are 'Religious Beliefs and Traditional Customs' and 'Insecure Communication System' which means rank are 3.32 and 3.31 respectively as shown above in the table 6.2. If the mean rank is higher, there is a greater constraint and if the mean rank is lower, there is a lesser constraint.

6.2 Descriptive Analysis of the Perception of Women Entrepreneurs on Banking Service

The banking sector plays a vital role for the development of women entrepreneurs in India. Several nationalized banks in India have special schemes for promoting entrepreneurship, especially for enterprises owned by women. The state and central governments also organize many training programmes for women entrepreneurs through the banking sectors. But due to the low awareness and the passive mindset there are only a very few takers. Though a number of credit schemes are available for women, there are several bottlenecks as well. There are some barriers between banking sectors and women entrepreneurs so that the bank schemes have not reached the women entrepreneurs properly. With better understanding of women entrepreneurs' perceptions, banks can determine the actions required to meet the women entrepreneurs' needs. Banks can identify their own strengths and weaknesses, chart out paths for future progress and improvement by analyzing the women entrepreneurs' perception.

The data collected were analyzed for the gaps under the major five headings, namely tangibles, reliability, assurance, responsiveness and empathy. Table 6.3 details the overall summary of the respondents' perception on the services provided by their banks on all the dimensions. This table includes the opinion of the respondents about their bank. Overall it can be inferred that approximately 75 per cent of the respondents have provided higher ratings, which implies that the respondents are satisfied about the various performance dimensions. At the same time it is also clear that there exists a huge scope for the improvisation of the performance dimensions.

Table 6.3

Overall Perceptions of Women Entrepreneurs on Banking Service

FACTORS	Very Poor	Poor	Moderate	Good	Very Good
TANGIBLES					
Parking Facilities	104 (27.37%)	152 (40%)	78 (20.53%)	30 (7.89%)	16 (4.21%)
Lighting	6 (1.58%)	17 (4.47%)	69 (18.16%)	214 (56.32%)	74 (19.47%)
Ventilation	23 (6.05%)	57 (15%)	249 (65.53%)	40 (10.53%)	11 (2.89%)
Drinking Water	197 (51.84%)	104 (27.37%)	52 (13.68%)	27 (7.11%)	0 (0%)
ATM Location	5 (1.32%)	74 (19.47%)	96 (25.26%)	198 (52.11%)	7 (1.84%)
Convenience of Banking Hours	13 (3.42%)	24 (6.32%)	67 (17.63%)	154 (40.53%)	122 (32.11%)
Availability of Challans and Forms	2 (0.52%)	10 (2.63%)	30 (7.89%)	112 (29.47%)	226 (59.47%)
RELIABILITY					
Understanding of Systems and Procedures	77 (20.26%)	163 (42.89%)	65 (17.11%)	43 (11.31%)	32 (8.42%)
Knowledge & Skill Level of Bank Officials	39 (10.26%)	82 (21.58%)	216 (56.84%)	32 (8.42%)	11 (2.89%)
ASSURANCE					
Attitude Level of Bank Officials	88 (23.16%)	142 (37.37%)	89 (23.42%)	43 (11.32%)	18 (4.74%)
Professional Approach of Bank Officials	72 (18.95%)	138 (36.32%)	108 (28.42%)	62 (16.32%)	0 (0%)
RESPONSIVENESS					
Handling and Response to Customer Complaints	143 (37.63%)	98 (25.79%)	120 (31.58%)	13 (3.42%)	6 (1.58%)
Man Power Availability	8 (2.11%)	30 (7.89%)	75 (19.74%)	153 (40.26%)	114 (30%)
EMPATHY					
Processing of Cheques	12 (3.16%)	34 (8.95%)	91 (23.95%)	156 (41.05%)	87 (22.89%)
Cash Deposit	9 (2.37%)	23 (6.05%)	98 (25.79%)	162 (42.63%)	88 (23.16%)
Processing of Loans	96 (25.26%)	172 (45.26%)	74 (19.47%)	30 (7.89%)	8 (2.11%)
Processing of Other Services	40 (10.53%)	164 (43.16%)	132 (34.74%)	32 (8.42%)	12 (3.16%)

The above table reveals that the majority of the respondents have poor perception in parking facilities (40 per cent), good perception in lighting (56.32 per cent), moderate perception in ventilation (65.53 per cent), very poor perception in drinking water (51.84 per cent), good perception in ATM location (52.11 per cent), good perception in convenience of banking hours (40.53 per cent) and very good perception in availability of challans and forms (59.47 per cent) under Tangibles Factor. In Reliability Factor, the majorities of the respondents have poor perception in under standing of systems and procedures (42.89 per cent) and moderate perception in the knowledge and skill level of bank officials (56.84 per cent). In Assurance Factor, the majority of the respondents have poor perception in the attitude level of bank officials (37.37 per cent) and in the professional approach (36.32 per cent) of bank officials. In Responsiveness Factor, the majority of the respondents have very poor perception in handling and response to customer complaints in the bank (37.63 per cent) and good perception in man power availability in the bank (40.26 per cent). In Empathy Factor, the majority of the respondents have good perception in processing of cheques (40.26 per cent) and cash deposit (42.63 per cent), poor perception in processing of loans (45.26 per cent) and poor processing of other services (43.16 per cent).

6.3 GAP Analysis of the Perception of Women Entrepreneurs on Banking Service

The raw data obtained on the expectations of the respondents on all the five dimensions of the quality, viz, tangibles, reliability, assurance, responsiveness and empathy were used to calculate the 'gap' that exists. This gap analysis was done for all the dimensions. Their levels were assessed purely on the basis of their mean values development comparing with a reference means value of '5' which was considered to be the maximum taking in the account that any organization should like to achieve for excellence. The gap i.e., the difference between the respondents score and the reference mean value is the 'service gap'. Table 6.4 details the service gap on all five dimensions of services.

Table 6.4

GAP Analysis of the Perceptions of Women Entrepreneurs on Banking Service

Dimensions	Expected Mean Score	Experienced Mean score	S.D	Service GAP
GAP ANALYSIS FOR TANGIBLES				
Parking Facilities	5	2.21	1.063	2.79
Lighting	5	3.88	0.827	1.12
Ventilation	5	2.89	0.777	2.11
Drinking Water	5	1.69	0.940	3.31
ATM Location	5	3.34	0.855	1.66
Convenience of Banking Hours	5	3.92	1.026	1.08
Availability of Challans and Forms	5	4.45	0.79	0.55
GAP ANALYSIS FOR RELIABILITY				
Understanding of Systems and Procedures	5	2.45	1.178	2.55
Knowledge and Skill Level	5	2.72	0.866	2.28
GAP ANALYSIS FOR ASSURANCE				
Attitude Level	5	3.37	1.100	1.63
Professional Approach	5	2.42	0.975	2.58
GAP ANALYSIS FOR RESPONSIVENESS				
Handling and Response to Customer Complaints	5	2.06	0.985	2.94
Man Power Availability	5	3.88	0.996	1.12
GAP ANALYSIS FOR EMPATHY				
Processing of Cheques	5	3.71	1.106	1.29
Cash Deposit	5	3.78	0.948	1.22
Processing of Loans	5	2.16	0.961	2.84
Processing of Other Services	5	2.51	0.906	2.49

A service gap of greater than 2.5 was considered to be highly critical area for the improvement of the performance dimensions. A service gap of less than 1.5 was treated as less significant and no need of treatment was required and a difference of 1.5 to 2.5 was considered as critical and it needed further improvement. It has been found that the drinking water facility (3.31), handling and response to respondents' complaints (2.94), processing of loans (2.84), parking facilities (2.79), professional approach (2.58), and understanding of systems and procedures (2.55) should be considered highly critical. The processing of other services (2.49), knowledge and skill level (2.28), ventilation (2.11), ATM location (1.66) and attitude level (1.63) are to be given critical consideration. The women entrepreneurs are satisfied with the processing of cheques (1.29), cash deposit (1.22), lighting (1.12), man power availability (1.12) convenience of banking hours (1.08) and availability of challans and forms (0.55) in the banks. On the whole it is found that a critical service gap exists in the tangibles, reliability, assurance, responsiveness and empathy dimensions. As it is seen from the table 6.4, all the factors in the above listed dimension which have a service gap of greater than 1.5 and greater than 2.5 ought to be considered critical and improvement of services on those factors are required.

The above table reveals that the majority of the women entrepreneurs have awarded least value to the tangibles. Among the factors, the drinking water facilities and the parking facility were rated the least by the women entrepreneurs followed by ventilation, ATM location and lighting of the banks. Similar to the tangibles, on the reliability and assurance dimensions, women entrepreneurs rated least on the services provided by the banks. On the reliability dimension, the women entrepreneurs are not satisfied with the understanding of systems and procedures of the bank. On the assurance dimension the women entrepreneurs are not satisfied with the professional approach of the employees and the attitude level of the bank. The same trend could also be found in the responsiveness dimension. The women entrepreneurs are not satisfied with the handling and response to customer complaints by the employees but they have satisfaction with the man power availability of the bank. On the empathy dimension, the women entrepreneurs are not satisfied with the processing of loans and processing of other services of bank but they have full satisfaction on the processing of cheques and cash deposit. The gap analysis reveals a critical distance on drinking water facility, handling and response to customer complaints, processing of loans, parking facility, professional approach and the employees' attitude, understanding of systems and procedure, processing of other services, knowledge and skill level and ventilation and improvements are required at vast level. Even though the availability of challans and forms in the bank is satisfactory, all the other factors on the five service dimensions need to be improved for better quality perception. The results here conclude that the performance delivery with respect to the banks has to be enhanced to leverage and improvise the level of service quality dimensions.

CHAPTER VII

SUMMARY OF FINDINGS, SUGGESTIONS AND CONCLUSION

The final chapter presents the findings of the study and lists down the various aspects and developments of women entrepreneurs in Tirunelveli district. It also includes the suggestions and conclusion of the study.

The objectives of the present study were accomplished in four stages. First of all, the profile of the women entrepreneurs and organizational profile of their enterprise were analyzed to understand the background of the women entrepreneurs. It was followed by the study on various developments among the women entrepreneurs through several development variables under the head of personality development, social development, personal development, innovational development, embankment development and intellectual development. It was carried out to analyze the level of development and its correlates. In the third stage, the analysis was carried out to analyze the different types of constraints faced by the women entrepreneurs during their enterprising. In the last stage, the analysis was carried out to analyze the perception of women entrepreneurs on banking services. The relationship between the women entrepreneurs and the officials of the banking sectors was also analyzed. Results of the analysis were presented and discussed in earlier chapters. The various steps of the study and its findings are summarized in this chapter to draw specific inferences and their policy implications.

The specific objectives of this study are:

I.   to know the profile and background of the respondents

II.   to bring out the organizational profile of the enterprises of the respondents

III.   to analyze the developments in personality, social, personal, innovational, embankment and intellectual of the respondents

IV.   to analyze various constraints faced by the women entrepreneurs to run their enterprise

V.   to study the overall perception of the respondents on banking service

VI.   to offer suitable suggestions based on the findings

The concepts and methodology were formulated according to the objectives of the study with the help of comprehensive reviews of previous studies. The secondary data about the women entrepreneurs were collected from the journals, books, websites and the district profile.

For primary data, 20 women entrepreneurs were identified from each block of Tirunelveli district. Since the district consists of 19 blocks, the total sample size was arbitrarily determined as 380. In each block, 20 entrepreneurs were identified with the help of known entrepreneurs, small traders associations and the local Panchayat-Union Presidents. The data were collected from the women entrepreneurs with the help of a structured interview schedule.

The collected data were analyzed with the help of appropriate tools to examine the profile of the women entrepreneurs, organizational profile of their enterprise, various developments, constraints faced by the women entrepreneurs and perception of the respondents on banking service. The various findings of the present study are summarized below:

7.1   MAJOR FINDINGS OF THE STUDY

7.1.1   Findings on the Personal Profile of the Women Entrepreneurs and the Organizational Profile of their Enterprises

1. 62.63 per cent of the women entrepreneurs do their business as sole proprietorship venture as women managed units in Tirunelveli district. 27.37 per cent and 10 per cent of the total respondents do their business with partnership such as jointly managed unit and men managed unit respectively.

2. The dominant age groups among the respondents are 36 to 45 years (26.58 per cent) and 46 to 55 years (25.79 per cent). The respondents who are in the group of 25 years and below and above 55 years are comparatively less in number.

3. The sample respondents are well educated and 36.05 per cent of the respondents are under graduate degree holders and 21.58 per cent of respondents are post graduates.

4. Regarding the marital status of respondents, married respondents dominate in all the categories with 56.31 per cent. A maximum of 77.63 per cent of the

total respondents belongs to the nuclear family system. 42.63 per cent of the total respondents have a family size of 3 to 4 members and 19.74 per cent have 5 to 6 family members.

5. The study also found that 49.21 per cent of the respondents have two earning members in the family and 20.53 per cent have only one earning member. 40 per cent of the respondents have Rs10001 to Rs15000 as personal income and 30 per cent of the respondents have Rs15001 to Rs20000 as personal income. The personal income of women managed unit respondents is higher than the income of other category respondents.

6. The occupational background among the respondents is entrepreneurs and private employees with 30.26 per cent and 28.42 per cent respectively. The occupational background of labourer is less quantity among the respondents. The other notable occupational backgrounds among the respondents are government employees and farmers.

7. A maximum of 53.42 per cent of the total respondents were house wives before starting their enterprise and 18.69 per cent of the respondents were unemployed. Minimum of the respondents were either students or in another enterprises.

8. 40.26 per cent of the respondents have not received any training so far and 22.63 per cent of the respondents underwent the training just before starting their business. Only a minimum number of respondents (8.95 per cent) got the training before and after starting the business.

9. Regarding the nature of enterprise, maximum of 26.84 per cent of the respondents run their enterprise related to services based and 25.79 per cent of the respondents run their enterprise related to manufacturing based. Most of the respondents engage themselves in printing and computer based jobs (41.05 per cent) and garments, textile and tailoring (25 per cent). A few number of respondents run beauty parlours (6.32 per cent).

10. The greater part of the respondents (36.85 per cent) has 10 to 12 employees in their enterprise, 29.47 per cent of the respondents have above 12 employees in

their enterprise. A few respondents (2.89 per cent) have 1 to 3 employees in their enterprise. 37.63 per cent of the respondents run their enterprise in their own premises. 28.16 per cent of the respondents run their enterprises in rented premises. 16.05 per cent of the respondents run their enterprises in leased premises.

11. A maximum of 46.84 per cent of the total respondents have 1 to 5 year old enterprises. Only 8.16 per cent of the total respondents have above 15 year old enterprises. Out of 380 respondents, the maximum of 37.37 per cent of the respondents have monthly turnover of above Rs1 to Rs3 lakh in their enterprise and 21.32 per cent of the respondents have monthly turnover of Rs1 lakh or less in their enterprise.

12. Majority of the respondents (37.63 per cent) get Rs20,001 to Rs30,000 as monthly profit in their enterprise followed by the respondents (27.11 per cent) who get Rs10,001 to Rs20,000 as monthly profit in their business.

13. A maximum of 38.68 per cent of the total respondents have become proprietors by created the enterprises themselves. 31.05 per cent of the total respondents have bought the enterprises from others, 18.16 per cent of the total respondents run their family enterprises (Inherited) and 8.95 per cent of the total respondents have leased one.

14. A maximum of 30.79 per cent of the total respondents have registered their enterprises in the District Industries Centre (DIC) at the time of bank loan and a minimum of 18.95 per cent of the total respondents have not registered their enterprises so far in the District Industries Centre (DIC).

15. Out of 380 respondents, the maximum of 42.63 per cent of the respondents have association membership with related trade association, 24.47 per cent of the respondents are members of other local associations, 16.32 per cent of the respondents have association membership with association of women entrepreneurs, 10.26 per cent of the respondents have association membership with self help groups and 6.32 per cent of the respondents do not have any association membership.

7.1.2   Findings on Various Developments of the Women Entrepreneurs

1. There is a significant development on the selected variables such as planning, information seeking, problem solving, confidence, honesty, faithfulness, persuasiveness, positive environment, social and family responsibilities, decreasing social barriers, financial, workplace, environmental, marketplace, values, managerial skill, best quality production, effective communication and negotiation, advertisement, discount & prizes, prompt delivery & supply, writing planning, money transaction through bank, using bank loan, prompt loan payback, prompt communication, accounting & auditing and examining the business network.

2. There is no significant development on some variables such as women business network, administrative and legal support, admiration at public places, assets, low margin, more sales & more profit, direct approach to the bank officials, avoiding mediators for loan, regular contact with bank officials, using mobile banking, internet usage, budget preparation and computerized work.

3. All categories of women entrepreneurs such as women managed unit, jointly managed unit and men managed unit have developed their personality development, personal development and innovational development.

4. Regarding the social development, only the women managed unit has developed it but the jointly managed unit and the men managed unit have not developed it.

5. Regarding the embankment development, the women managed unit and the jointly managed unit have developed it but the men managed unit has not developed it.

6. Regarding the intellectual development, the women managed unit and the jointly managed unit have developed it but the men managed unit has not developed it.

7. The first factor 'Personality Development' is a linear combination of seven variables namely, planning, information seeking, problem solving, confidence, honesty, faithfulness and persuasiveness. These seven variables have high loadings on Factor I. The variable 'Planning' has the highest loading on the

factor personality development. The factor has Eigen value 95.478 which explains 67.383 pre cent of the variance.

8. The second factor 'Social Development' comprises of six variables namely, positive environment, family and social responsibilities, decreasing social barriers, women business network, administrative and legal support and environment at public places. These variables have high loadings on Factor II which can be called 'Social Development'. The variable 'Women Business Network' has the highest loading on the factor social development. Its Eigen value is 14.431 and it explains 10.184 per cent of the total variance.

9. The third Factor 'Personal Development' captures the core of these seven variables namely, assets development, financial development, workplace development, environmental development, marketplace development, values development and managerial skill development. The variable 'Values Development' has the highest loading on the factor personal development. Its Eigen value is 12.221 and it explains 8.625 per cent of the total variance.

10. The fourth Factor 'Innovational Development' captures the heart of these seven variables namely, low margin, more sales and more profit, best quality production, effective communication and negotiation skills, advertisement, discount and prizes, prompt delivery and supply and writing planning. The variable 'Low Margin, More Sales and More Profit' has the highest loading on the factor innovational development. Its Eigen value is 9.642 and it explains 6.805 per cent of the total variance.

11. The fifth Factor 'Embankment Development' is a linear combination of seven variables namely, money transaction through bank, using bank loan, direct approach to the bank officials, avoiding the mediators for loan, prompt loan payback, regular contact with bank officials and using mobile banking. These seven variables have high loadings on Factor V. The variable 'Avoiding the Mediators for Loan' has the highest loading on the factor embankment development. The factor has Eigen value 5.749 which explains 4.057 per cent of the variance.

12. The sixth Factor 'Intellectual Development' captures the heart of six variables namely, internet usage, prompt communication, maintenance of accounting, budget preparation, examining the business network and computerized work. The variable 'Examining the Business Network' has the highest loading on the factor intellectual development. Its Eigen value is 4.173 and it explains 2.945 per cent of the total variance.

13. The development factors namely, personality development, social development, personal development, innovational development, embankment development and intellectual development have loadings of 0.561, 0.768, 0.860, 0.895, 0.771 and 0.866 respectively. There Eigen values are 95.478, 14.431, 12.221, 9.642, 5.749 and 4.173 respectively and they explain 67.383, 10.184, 8.625, 6.805, 4.057 and 2.945 per cent of the total variance respectively.

14. The correlation coefficient result proves that the various development factors of the women entrepreneurs are significantly highly correlated, inter linked and inter dependent.

15. There is a significant difference among the mean rank of variables of personality development, social development, personal development, innovational development, embankment development and intellectual development.

16. There is a significant difference among the mean rank of factors of personality development, social development, personal development, innovational development, embankment development and intellectual development. Post-hoc test reveals that there is a significant difference between all the combination except the combination of personal development and embankment development and personal development and intellectual development.

7.1.3 Findings on Constraints Faced By the Women Entrepreneurs

1. The constraint such as health problems, gender discriminations, social barriers, insecure communication system, religious beliefs & traditional customs, family restriction, sexual harassment and multiple roles of the women entrepreneurs

have high loadings of 0.930, 0.929, 0.924, 0.924, 0.918, 0.906, 0.905 and 0.851 respectively.

2. Other constraints such as marketing competitions with males and negative attitudes of society have low loadings of 0.466 and 0.272 respectively. There is a significant difference among the mean rank variables of constraints faced by the women entrepreneurs.

3. As far as the mean rank of various constraints is concerned, the women entrepreneurs suffer very much the constraints such as social barriers, health problems, marketing competitions with males, sexual harassment, multiple roles, negative attitudes of the society and gender discriminations.

4. The present study also has found that the constraints of family restriction, religious beliefs & traditional customs and insecure communication system do not affect the women entrepreneurs much.

7.1.4 Findings on Perception of Women Entrepreneur on Banking Service

1. The banking services of drinking water facility, handling and response to customer complaints, processing of loans, parking facilities, professional approach, and understanding of systems & procedures should be considered highly critical area for the improvement of the performance dimensions.

2. The processing of other services, knowledge and skill level, ventilation, ATM location and attitude level of the banking services are to be given critical consideration and further needs for improvements.

3. The women entrepreneurs are satisfied with the processing of cheques, cash deposit, lighting, man power availability, banking hours and availability of challans and forms in the banks.

4. Majority of the women entrepreneurs has awarded least value to the tangibles. Among the factors, the drinking water facilities and the parking facility were rated the least by the women entrepreneurs followed by ventilation, ATM location and lighting of the banks.

5. Similar to the tangibles, on the reliability, women entrepreneurs rated least on the services provided by the banks. On the reliability dimension the women entrepreneurs are not satisfied with the understanding of systems & procedures of the bank.

6. In the assurance dimension, the women entrepreneurs are not satisfied with the professional approach of the employees and the attitude level of the bank.

7. The same trend could also be found in the responsiveness dimension. The women entrepreneurs are not happy about the handling & response to customer complaints by the employees but they appreciate man power availability of the bank.

8. In the empathy dimension, the women entrepreneurs do not like the way of processing of loans and processing of other services of bank but they do not complain about the processing of cheques and cash deposit.

7.2   SUGGESTIONS

In the changed environment, the women entrepreneurs in small scale industries need to integrate themselves with the overall domestic economic and global marketing by gearing themselves to greater independence and by networking and sub contracting. Building competitive strengths, introducing technology up gradation and quality improvement in their enterprises are the vital issues which need to be addressed in order to build the capability to withstand emerging pressures and to ensure sustained growth. The following suggestions are given on the basis of the result of the study in order to overcome the hurdles, to face the constraints and to elevate the socio-economic status of women, which in turn will lead to the economic growth and overall development of the district, state and nation.

1. In Tirunelveli district, the potentialities of women entrepreneurs are not properly identified. Hence the Government and NGOs should conduct programmes to identify the potentialities of women who could become successful entrepreneurs so that cent per cent of women managed unit can be generated.

2. The majority of the respondents are above 35 years of age so the training and retraining of women over 35 years is important. Such training programmes should include the psychology of doing business, new dimensions of life skills for business, building self-esteem, negotiation skills, marketing, international competition, etc.

3. The district has well educated women entrepreneurs. Education has been instrumental in increasing the participation of women in entrepreneurial activities. Good academic background makes women confident in dealing with problems in business in an effective manner. Education is a powerful tool in breaking down the barriers to successful entrepreneurship. Government should provide better educational facilities and schemes to women folk.

4. As most of the women entrepreneurs are married and most of them live in nuclear families with 3 – 4 members, husbands and men folk should be made to realize the significance of women entrepreneurship. Then, their attitude, role and expectation will change and they will provide the necessary capital, guidance and moral support to the women entrepreneurs.

5. The personal income of the women entrepreneurs is not appreciable in the study area. Income generating activities should be introduced and developed among the women entrepreneurs.

6. The untrained women entrepreneurs are more than trained ones in the district. There is a need for training the already existing women entrepreneurs in the various aspects of management. The Government must make genuine efforts to publicize the various schemes announced from time to time to attract women entrepreneurs who have not undergone the training so far.

7. Even though some of the respondents are running their family enterprise (Inherited), they should shift from the traditional sectors of entrepreneurship and adhere to the modern trend in order to earn more.

7.2.1 Suggestions to Personality Development

1. Training in entrepreneurial attitudes should be started for women at the high school level through well-designed courses, which will build their confidence

level and enable them to prepare a plan, seeking information, solving problems and honesty, faithfulness and persuasiveness will be achieved through behavioral games.

2. Women training programme should be organized to encourage more passive women entrepreneurs. They should be taught to recognize their own psychological needs and express them.

3. Counseling through the aid of committed NGOs, psychologists, managerial experts and technical personnel should be provided to the existing and emerging women entrepreneurs.

4. Training and counseling on a large scale for existing women entrepreneurs should be organized to remove psychological factors like lack of self-confidence, lack of planning, lack of problem solving and fear of success.

5. There should be an incessant attempt to motivate, give confidence, inspire and assist women entrepreneurs.

6. To improve their over-all personality standards, personality development training should be arranged and after such programmes, continuous monitoring and practical exercises should be given.

7. Proper training institutes for women entrepreneurs should be established for enhancing their level of business planning, work-knowledge, skills, risk-taking abilities and enhancing their capabilities. Training centres should provide training to prospective women entrepreneurs free of cost and entrepreneurship development programmes should be much more practical oriented. Inculcation of self-confidence amongst women should be one of the prime motives of these programmes.

8. The elaboration of a business plan by new women entrepreneurs should be encouraged by lending institutions and entrepreneurs. Organizations such as DIC, SIPCOT and the planning division of the entrepreneurs have to assist women entrepreneurs in this regard. It is important that these organizations should guide potential women entrepreneurs.

7.2.2 Suggestions to Social Development

1. Positive attitudinal change in the society recognizing the role of women as entrepreneurs may lead to the development of appropriate environment in which women will be able to exhibit their entrepreneurial talents.

2. A women entrepreneur should herself set up an example in the society by being successful and should act as a role model. Since children have a tendency to emulate their parents, the resultant effect would be automatic.

3. The most critical factor here is recognition in the society. The existence of the women entrepreneurs first of all need to be recognized. Secondly, they need to be recognized as a group contributing towards the economic growth and development of the country. To achieve this, they need the support of the Central Government, State Government, Donors, Non-Governmental Agencies, Women's Networks, national Corporate Organizations and national Entrepreneurs. As long as these women entrepreneurs are not recognized and given the priority, their economic potential and entrepreneurial capacity will remain undermined.

4. Role models can be used as a source of inspiration for girls and women. Successful women entrepreneurs or other prominent women could, for example, be invited to give lectures. The introduction of an annual award to honour a woman who excels in business may also be considered.

5. In order to promote the organization and networking of women entrepreneurs with like interests, key organizations may designate a coordinator, whose responsibility would be to first identify existing groupings of women entrepreneurs. The coordinator should furthermore assist in the strengthening of existing groupings and if necessary, help in the formation of new associations. The coordinator may also provide a reference to other relevant institutions for information, training and assistance to interested women entrepreneurs.

6. The establishment of a mentor system should be considered. Through such a system, successful businesswomen could be matched with other businesswomen

to share experiences and develop a network of women business owners. NGOs and business associations should prevent the backstopping of such an initiative.

7. Entrepreneurs should keep abreast of the knowledge about new techniques, financial institutions, training institutions and marketing linkages. Some agencies working for women entrepreneurs are:

    a. SISI (Small Industry Service Institute)

    b. DIC (District Industry Centre)

    c. STEP (Science and Technology Entrepreneurship Park)

    d. Behavioural Science Centres

    e. Indian Institute of Technology (Delhi)

7.2.3 Suggestions to Personal Development

1. Organizations that provide services to small scale industries and organizations with the aim of raising the status of women should train potential women entrepreneurs in personal development and in their attitudes towards business.

2. Women have a tendency to allow men to register assets in their name despite the fact that the woman may have contributed to their acquisition. There is a need to sensitize women and men about the advantages of registering assets in both the names.

3. Creating provision of micro credit system and enterprise credit system to the women entrepreneurs at local level should be encouraged.

4. Offering seed capital, up-lift schemes, women entrepreneurs fund etc. should be developed to encourage them economically.

5. Provision should be made to provide land and sheds to deserving women entrepreneurs on priority basis. Group Women Entrepreneurship (GWE) may be promoted in rural sector by reinvigorating activities and skills on traditional crafts or practices with which they are acquainted.

6. Pollution control department could organize a training or workshop on pollution control and environmental development to the women entrepreneurs.

7. Safety in the work place is important. Machines, chemicals and other raw materials (i.e. oils, paints, etc.) used for the production should be stored safely, kept under control and put out of reach of children's hands. This may be relevant especially for home-based manufacturing where children are around.

8. Adequate training programmes on managerial skills and business ethics should be conducted to women entrepreneurs.

9. Women's participation in decision-making should be encouraged.

10. Industrial estates could also provide marketing outlets for the display and sale of products made by women entrepreneurs.

7.2.4 Suggestions to Innovational Development

1. The study reveals that Low margin, More Sales & More Profit is not a successful one in the study area and it will not bring success in all times in the business. It is also one of the risky techniques for women entrepreneurs. It is suggested only for women entrepreneurs who have more capital in business to use this innovational technique.

2. It is a common fact that all customers like to purchase best quality products. It is the responsibility of a company to give products of best quality for the customers. At the same time the degree of quality will vary according to the economic status of the people. The women entrepreneurs are recommended that they have to study the economic status of the area where the enterprise is to be initiated to fix the quality condition of the product.

3. Government organization could organize a training progaramme with the help of specialists on communication and negotiation skills to the women entrepreneurs for their business development.

4. With regard to lack of customers and competition and marketing the most common solution proposed is advertising. Strategically placed proper advertising is suggested to the women entrepreneurs.

5. The discount and prizes is the best innovational technique as well as good advertisement to uplift the business when the net margin decreases. The respondents are suggested that they could use this technique on either festival period or specific period.

6. The way of distributing the products and delivering services involves both the cost factor and the clients' satisfaction factor. Transportation of goods to a shop or a client can be done by air, sea, rail or road. Each method of transportation has its advantages and disadvantages depending on timeframe, volume, access to suppliers and cost. The respondents are suggested that they have to concentrate on prompt delivery and supply.

7. The respondents should begin the process of preparing action plan by focusing on a few key elements: i) to establish the basic business goals, ii) to determine what challenges and opportunities the business may face, iii) to identify clearly the target markets and competition and iv) to consider and plan all the operational and financial requirements needed to achieve the goals.

7.2.5 Suggestions to Embankment Development

1. In order to increase the embankment development for women entrepreneurs, it has been suggested a) to organize an awareness programme on banking sector among the women entrepreneurs; b) to appoint women managers in banks to deal with women entrepreneurs. This would remove the inhabitation of the women entrepreneurs and would resist the mediators; c) to advocate for awareness-raising amongst banking staff towards women's higher re-payment rates, and advocate for more female staff working in micro finance institutions. This would increase mutual trust between women entrepreneurs and the bankers and therefore generate a more comfortable and conducive environment for women entrepreneurs within the banking system; and d) to conduct micro finance awareness raising training, which would combine the topics on how to access micro finance and the benefits and procedures connected with it. This would take away the mysteriousness of micro finance, and therefore decrease the fear of women entrepreneurs related to micro finance.

7.2.6   Suggestions to Intellectual Development

1. In modern era, mobile banking is unavoidable for every individual especially entrepreneurs. But in the study area the women entrepreneurs have no significant development in mobile banking. The banking sector should take necessary steps to implement the mobile banking schemes for women entrepreneurs.

2. The women entrepreneurs should be given training in bookkeeping and cash management, since many have no formal methods for the good management of their receipts and expenditure and are therefore not able to rightly judge the profit or loss, of their business. Such training also requires follow-up to ensure that entrepreneurs keep track of their business developments.

3. Without a budget in business is like a journey towards an unknown village. The respondents should learn the management skills such as budgeting and accounting and auditing through various training programmes organized by the management institutions. Adequate training programmes on management skills should be provided to women entrepreneurs.

4. More than 50 per cent of the women entrepreneurs in the study area are computer illiterates. They are not aware of how information technology can help them shorten business processes, improve product quality, communicate by e-mail, study the business network, improve customer service and increase marketability of their products and services. These women need to be trained on the benefits of technology and internet.

5. Banking sectors should provide a special loan for women entrepreneurs for purchasing computers. A 'Soft Skills Training Institute' would greatly enhance the computer skills of these women entrepreneurs and improve their productivity and profitability.

7.2.7   Suggestions to overcome the constraints

1. Women entrepreneurs have faced many health problems such as tension, backache, eyestrain, fatigue and headache. In order to overcome these problems, they should involve in regular physical exercise, yoga and meditation.

2. When women work outside their homes, they face the problem of dual role and they are in a conflicting frame of mind whether to give priority to home or career. Hence, their partners and other family members should share the household activities.

3. Organizations should also consider employing of female business advisors or hiring of advisory services of successful businesswomen, since several sources indicate that factors outside the business such as family circumstances, gender discrimination, negative attitude of the society, social barriers and sexual harassment may affect the performance of the business. Women may be willing to discuss these matters with other women. The advisors or businesswomen can provide advice and warn them of the pitfalls.

4. A women entrepreneur's guidance cell should be set up to handle various problems of women entrepreneurs all over the district.

5. In the district, there is no association of women entrepreneurs. They can form an association and meet at a central place on a regular basis so as to discuss their needs, problems, experiences and achievements.

6. Self-help groups must be formulated to overcome the common entrepreneurial problems.

7.2.8 Suggestions to Banking Sectors

1. Even though the respondents appreciate the availability of challans & forms in the bank, all the other factors on the five service dimensions need to be improved for better quality perception. It is suggested that the performance delivery of the banks has to be enhanced to leverage and improvise the level of service quality dimensions.

2. Though the respondents are aware of the banking procedures to get loan, they feel that the procedures are complicated and time consuming. Hence, the procedure and formalities of the bank should be simplified and the required documents should be minimized. Moreover, all the documents should be in regional language.

3. Repeated gender sensitization programmes should be held to train bank officials to treat women with dignity and respect.

4. Banks should have a thorough knowledge about the different types of businesses and their specific banking necessities. The bankers ask for reimbursement too quickly and do not understand that the money is tied up in the business during the start-up period. It is suggested that bankers should get rid of their negative attitude towards women entrepreneurs and should give sufficient time for them to repay the loan.

5. Finance is sine-qua-non for any enterprise. The banking system is not sufficiently responsive to social banking needs and has not been able to deal with barriers that hinder women from using or gaining access to credit. Adequate arrangements must be made for the supply of credit facility at concession rate for the women entrepreneurs in view of their growing needs.

7.3 CONCLUSION

India is a male dominated society and women are assumed to be economically as well as socially dependent on male members. The absolute dependence seems to be diluted among the high and middle class women as they become aware of personal needs and demand absolute equality.

Women entrepreneurs face lots of problems at their personal as well as entrepreneurial development. Technological advancement and information technology explosion have reduced the problem of women entrepreneurs to a great extent. But the mental revolution of the society is needed to change the attitude of the society and provide women with democratic and entrepreneurial platform.

Moreover with increasing assistance from Government, Non-Government and other financial institutions for various women entrepreneurs, there can be significant increase brought about in the growth of women entrepreneurship process. Still efforts are being made to coordinate with the enterprise activities of women providing them with utmost financial, morale, psychological support by various institutions working within the country and world-wide.

The small scale industries are considered as ideal nurseries for the rapid growth and development of women entrepreneurs. The need of the hour is the growth of women entrepreneurs in the country to accelerate the process of economic growth. From the point of view of long-term perspective, however, the capacity of small scale industries to become economically viable, technically progressive and efficient and to develop competitive strength shall be the only justification for their continuance. In the present study, an attempt has been made to assess the personal and occupational profiles, various developments, various constraints and perception on banking services of women entrepreneurs on small scale industries in Tirunelveli District.

The present study will help the planners and the decision makers who are involved in the development of women entrepreneurs in small scale industries to review the existing policies and to make suitable suggestions to amend the provisions of the act which governs the small scale industries. Based on the experience of the researcher the following important issues have been identified for an in depth study. The researcher will feel amply rewarded if the present study helps to undertake similar studies in the areas suggested below.

1. A study on the impact of Government Schemes for the development and promotion of women entrepreneurs in Small Scale Industries.

2. Constraints on Women Entrepreneurship Development in Tamil Nadu: An analysis of familial, social, and psychological dimensions.

3. A Study on Quality of Service of Banking Sector as a Tool for Enhancement of Women Entrepreneurs in Small Scale Industries.

4. An analysis of the factors responsible for the slow growth of women entrepreneurs in Small Scale Industries.

5. A study of the factors causing sickness of women entrepreneurs in Small Scale Industries.

It is hoped that the suggestions forwarded in the study will help the entrepreneurs in particular and policy-planners in general to look into this problem and develop better schemes, developmental programmes and opportunities to the women folk to enter into entrepreneurial ventures. It is also hoped that future research will feature an extensive quantitative survey of entrepreneurs in different locations throughout Tamil Nadu.

It is believed that women have the potential and the determination to set up, uphold and supervise their own enterprises in a very systematic manner. Appropriate encouragement from the society in general and family members in particular is required to help these women scale new heights in their business ventures. The right kind of assistance from family, society and Government can make these women entrepreneurs a part of the mainstream of national economy and they can contribute to the economic progress of India.

The study is concluded with the words which emphasize the development of women entrepreneurs. Individually, business ownership provides women with the independence they crave and with economic and social success they need. Nationally, business ownership has great importance for future economic prosperity. Globally, women are enhancing, directing, and changing the face of how business is done today. Ultimately, female business owners must be recognized for who they are, what they do, and how significantly they impact the world's global economy.

INTERVIEW SCHEDULE

Personal Profile of Women Entrepreneur

1. Type of Ownership : Women Managed Units (WMU) / Jointly Managed Units (JMU) / Men Managed Units (MMU).

2. Age : 25 and below / 26 – 35 / 36 – 45 / 46 – 55 / above 55

3. Educational Level : SSLC / Higher Secondary Level / U G Level / P G Level / Technical

4. Marital Status : Unmarried / Recently Married / Married / Widow / Separated

5. Nature of the Family : Nuclear / Joint

6. Size of the Family : Below 3 / 3 – 4 / 5 – 6 / 7 – 8 / above 8

7. Earning members in Family : One / Two / Three / Four / More than Four

8. Personal Income per month : 10000 or less / 10001 – 15000 / 15001 – 20000 / 20001 – 25000 / More than 25000

9. Occupational background : Labourer / Farmer / Government Employee / Private Employee / Entrepreneur

10. Position before starting the Enterprise : Student / Unemployed / Employed / House wife / In Another Enterprise

11. Occasion of the Training Programme : Before starting the enterprise/ At the time of starting the enterprise/ After starting the enterprise/ Before and after starting the enterprise/ No Training so far

Organization Profile of the Women Entrepreneurs

12.   Nature of the Enterprise

1. Manufacturing ☐   2. Repairing and Maintenance ☐

3. Trading ☐   4. Services ☐   5. Others ☐

13.   Types of the Sector

1. Garments, Textile & Tailoring ☐   2. Printing & Computers based ☐

3. Beauty Parlour ☐   4. Dairy Farming & Poultry ☐   5. Others ☐

14.   Number of Employees   : 1 – 3 / 4 – 6 / 7 – 9 / 10 – 12 / Above 12

15.   Nature of Premises of

the Enterprise   : Owned / Partially Owned / Rented / Leased / Others

16.   Age of Enterprise   : Below 1 y / 1-5 y / 6-10 y /11-15 y /above 15 y

17.   Monthly Turnover   : Rs1 lakh or less / above Rs1 lakh-Rs3 lakh / above Rs3
                                        lakh-Rs5 lakh / above Rs5 lakh-Rs7 lakh /above Rs7
                                        lakh

18.   Monthly Profit   : Rs10000 or less / Rs10001 – Rs20000 / Rs20001 –
                                        Rs30,000 / Rs30,001 – Rs40,000 / above Rs40,000

19.   Mode of creation (History of enterprise)

1. Enterprise Created by self ☐   2. Family enterprise (Inherited) ☐

3. Enterprise, which has been Bought ☐   4. Leased ☐   5. Others ☐

20   Time of Registration in District Industry Center

1. After starting the enterprise ☐   2. At the time of starting the enterprise ☐

3. At the time Bank Loan ☐   4. Before starting the enterprise ☐

5. Not Yet Registered ☐

21.   Membership in Association

1. Related Trade Association ☐   2. Other Local Association ☐

3. Association of Women Entrepreneurs ☐   4. Self Help Groups ☐   5. None ☐

Personality Development of Women Entrepreneurs

22.

Planning	Always	Usually	Some-times	Never	No idea
I think logically about what I am doing and what I am going to do.					
I try to foresee possible obstacles when I am making plans.					
I do not plan on the assumption that all will go well. I anticipate and plan for problems.					
I try to plan how I will get over difficulties before they actually happen.					

23.

Information Seeking	Always	Usually	Some-times	Never	No idea
Myself I find out what I need to know.					
When I am going to do something, first of all I make some inquires to find out how to do it.					
I make extensive methodical inquires about how to do things.					
If a problem needs to be analyzed, I analyze it myself.					

24.

Problem Solving	Always	Usually	Some-times	Never	No idea
If there are several alternatives, I think carefully about each one of them before I make my decision.					
I find solution for the problems which other people have failed to find.					
I find innovative solutions to problems.					
I develop new ideas.					

25.

Confidence	Always	Usually	Some-times	Never	No idea
I believe I can overcome obstacles.					
I know I can do what I set out to do.					
When I start a task I am confident that I can complete it.					
If I meet a challenge I believe I can overcome it.					

26.

Honesty	Always	Usually	Some-times	Never	No idea
I keep my word even if it hurts.					
I do not make promises I cannot keep.					
I do not accept or pay bribes or kickbacks to get what I want.					
People trust me with their money					

27.

Faithfulness	Always	Usually	Some-times	Never	No idea
I am willing to suffer a loss of money to maintain a relationship.					
I do not neglect my responsibilities as a spouse, parent or friend for the sake of my business or work activity.					
I maintain a close relationship with God even when I am very busy.					
I am willing to sacrifice my own interest to see another person benefit.					

28.

Persuasiveness	Always	Usually	Some-times	Never	No idea
I am good at convincing people to buy things.					
If I want somebody to do something for me, I can usually persuade him/her to do it.					
When I need people to do a task for me, I can made them do it.					
I can persuade people to do things for me because they trust me.					

Social Development of the Respondent

Q.No	Social Development	Very Good	Good	Moderate	Poor	Very Poor
29	Overall a positive environment for women to enter into business has been ensured					
30	Social and family responsibilities to promote women in business have increased					
31	Social barriers are decreased					
32	Women business network is extended					
33	Women are getting administrative and legal support					
34	Admiration at the public Places					

Personal Development of Women Entrepreneurs

I.   Assets Development
(Development between the time of starting the business till now)

Q.No	Assets (Amount in Rupees)	Below 25 %	25 %	50 %	75 %	Above 75 %
35.	Lands					
36.	Buildings					
37.	Machinery and Tools / Materials					
38.	Vehicles					
39.	Jewels					
40.	House Hold Properties					

II.   Financial Development
(Development between the time of starting the business till now)

Q.No	Finance (Amount in Rupees)	Below 25 %	25 %	50 %	75 %	Above 75 %
41.	Own Funds					
42.	Investment					
43.	Borrowed Funds					
44.	Cash in Hands					
45.	Cash at Banks					
46.	Savings per month					

III.   Workplace Development

47.   Do you encourage your employees to develop real skills and long-term careers (e.g. Via a performance appraisal process, a training plan)?

Always □   Frequently □ Need based □   Occasionally □   No □

48.   Is there a process to ensure that adequate steps are taken against all forms of discrimination, both in the workplace and at the time of recruitment (e.g. Against women, ethnic groups, disabled people, etc.)?

Always □   Frequently □   Need based □   Occasionally □   No □

49.   Do you consult with employees on important issues?

Always □   Frequently □   Need based □   Occasionally □   No □

50.   Does your enterprise have suitable arrangements for health, safety and welfare that provide sufficient protection for your employees?

Fully □   Maximum □   Partly □   Occasionally □   No □

51. Does your enterprise actively offer a good work-life balance for its employees, for example, by considering flexible working hours or allowing employees to work at home?

Always ☐　　Frequently ☐　　Need based ☐　　Occasionally ☐　　No ☐

IV. Environmental Development

52. Have you tried to reduce your enterprise's environmental impact in energy conservation?

Always ☐　　Frequently ☐　Need based ☐　　Occasionally ☐　　No ☐

53. Have you tried to reduce your enterprise's environmental impact in waste minimization and recycling?

Always ☐　　Frequently ☐　　Need based ☐　　Occasionally ☐　　No ☐

54. Have you tried to reduce your enterprise's environmental impact in pollution prevention (e.g. Emissions to air and water, effluent discharges, noise)?

Always ☐　　Frequently ☐　　Need based ☐　　Occasionally ☐　　No ☐

55. Have you tried to reduce your enterprise's environmental impact in the protection of the natural environment?

Always ☐　　Frequently ☐　　Need based ☐　　Occasionally ☐　　No ☐

56. Have you tried to reduce your enterprise's environmental impact in sustainable transport options?

Always ☐　　Frequently ☐　　Need based ☐　　Occasionally ☐　　No ☐

V. Marketplace Development

57. Does your company have a policy to ensure honesty and quality in all its contracts, dealings and advertising (e.g. a fair purchasing policy, provisions for consumer protection, etc)?

Always ☐　　Frequently ☐　Need based ☐　　Occasionally ☐　　No ☐

58. Does your enterprise supply clear and accurate information and labelling about products and services, including its after-sales obligations?

Always ☐　　Frequently ☐　Need based ☐　　Occasionally ☐　　No ☐

59. Does your business ensure timely payment of suppliers' invoices?

Always ☐　　Frequently ☐　Need based ☐　　Occasionally ☐　　No ☐

60. Does your company have a process to ensure effective feedback, consultation and/or dialogue with customers, suppliers and other people you do business with?

Always ☐　　Frequently ☐　Need based ☐　　Occasionally ☐　　No ☐

61. Does your enterprise register and resolve complaints from customers, suppliers and business partners?

 Always ☐ Frequently ☐ Need based ☐ Occasionally ☐ No ☐

VI. Values Development

62. Have you clearly defined your enterprise's values and rules of conduct?

 Always ☐ Frequently ☐ Need based ☐ Occasionally ☐ No ☐

63. Do you communicate your enterprise's values to customers, business partners, suppliers and other interested parties (e.g. in sales presentations, marketing material or informal communication)?

 Always ☐ Frequently ☐ Need based ☐ Occasionally ☐ No ☐

64. Are your customers aware of your enterprise's values and rules of conduct?

 Always ☐ Frequently ☐ Need based ☐ Occasionally ☐ No ☐

65. Are your employees aware of your enterprise's values and rules of conduct?

 Always ☐ Frequently ☐ Need based ☐ Occasionally ☐ No ☐

66. Do you train employees on the importance of your enterprise's values and rules of conduct?

 Always ☐ Frequently ☐ Need based ☐ Occasionally ☐ No ☐

VII. Managerial Skill Development

67. How do you think about yourself?

 Inevitable ☐ Active ☐ Passive ☐ Waste ☐ No Idea ☐

68. How do you feel about your task?

 Several Tasks ☐ Individual Task ☐ Moderate Task ☐ Combined Task ☐ No Task ☐

69. Are you willing to give power to others?

 Always ☐ Frequently ☐ Need based ☐ Occasionally ☐ No ☐

70. Do you share your information with others?

 Always ☐ Frequently ☐ Need based ☐ Occasionally ☐ No ☐

71. How do you pay rewards?

 Seniority Based ☐ Task Based ☐ Need based ☐ Relation Based ☐ No rewards ☐

Innovational Development

Q.No	Variables	Highly Needed	Needed	Moderately Needed	Not Needed	Definitely Not Needed
72.	Low Margin, More Sales & More Profit					
73.	Best Quality Production					
74.	Effective Communication and Negotiation Skills					
75.	Advertisement					
76.	Discount and Prizes					
77.	Prompt Delivery & Supply					
78.	Preparing Action plan					

Embankment Development

79. Money Transaction through Bank

Always □   Frequently □   Need based □   Occasionally □   No □

80. Using Bank Loan with subsidy

Always □   Frequently □   Need based □   Occasionally □   No □

81. Direct Approach to the Bank Officials

Always □   Frequently □   Need based □   Occasionally □   No □

82. Avoiding Mediators for Loan

Always □   Frequently □   Need based □   Occasionally □   No □

83. Prompt Repayment of the Loan

Always □   Frequently □   Need based □   Occasionally □   No □

84. Regular Contact with Bank Officials

Always □   Frequently □   Need based □   Occasionally □   No □

85. Using Mobile Banking

Always □   Frequently □   Need based □   Occasionally □   No □

Intellectual Development

86. Internet Usage

    Always ☐   Frequently ☐   Need based ☐   Occasionally ☐   No ☐

87. Prompt Communication

    Always ☐   Frequently ☐   Need based ☐   Occasionally ☐   No ☐

88. Accounting & Auditing

    Always ☐   Frequently ☐   Need based ☐   Occasionally ☐   No ☐

89. Budget Preparation

    Always ☐   Frequently ☐   Need based ☐   Occasionally ☐   No ☐

90. Examining the Business Network

    Always ☐   Frequently ☐   Need based ☐   Occasionally ☐   No ☐

91. Computerized Work

    Always ☐   Frequently ☐   Need based ☐   Occasionally ☐   No ☐

Constrains of Women Entrepreneurs

Obstacles / Problems for Running the Business

Q.No	Obstacles / Problems	Very High	High	Moderate	Low	Very Low
92.	Multiple roles of the women entrepreneurs					
93.	Marketing competitions with males					
94.	Gender discrimination					
95.	Negative attitudes of the society towards women in business					
96.	Health problems					
97.	Social barriers					
98.	Insecure communication system					
99.	Sexual harassment					
100.	Family restriction					
101.	Religious beliefs and traditional customs					

Overall Perceptions of Women Entrepreneurs about Banking Service

TANGIBLES

102. Parking Facilities in the Bank

Very Poor □   Poor □   Moderate □   Good □   Very Good □

103. Lighting in the Bank

Very Poor □   Poor □   Moderate □   Good □   Very Good □

104. Ventilation in the Bank

Very Poor □   Poor □   Moderate □   Good □   Very Good □

105. Drinking water in the Bank

Very Poor □   Poor □   Moderate □   Good □   Very Good □

106. ATM location of the Bank

Very Poor □   Poor □   Moderate □   Good □   Very Good □

107. Convenience of Banking Hours

Very Poor □   Poor □   Moderate □   Good □   Very Good □

108. Availability of Challans & Forms in the Bank

Very Poor □   Poor □   Moderate □   Good □   Very Good □

RELIABILITY

109. Understanding of systems & Procedures in the Bank

Very Poor □   Poor □   Moderate □   Good □   Very Good □

110. Knowledge & Skill Level of Bank Officials

Very Poor □   Poor □   Moderate □   Good □   Very Good □

ASSURANCE

111. Attitude level of Bank Officials

Very Poor □   Poor □   Moderate □   Good □   Very Good □

112. Professional Approach of Bank Officials

Very Poor □   Poor □   Moderate □   Good □   Very Good □

RESPONSIVENESS

113. Handling & Response to Customer Complaints in the Bank

Very Poor □   Poor □   Moderate □   Good □   Very Good □

114. Man Power availability in the Bank

Very Poor □   Poor □   Moderate □   Good □   Very Good □

EMPATHY

115. Processing of Cheques in the Bank

   Very Poor □   Poor □   Moderate □   Good □   Very Good □

116. Cash Deposit in the Bank

   Very Poor □   Poor □   Moderate □   Good □   Very Good □

117. Processing of Loans in the Bank

   Very Poor □   Poor □   Moderate □   Good □   Very Good □

118. Processing of other services in the Bank

   Very Poor □   Poor □   Moderate □   Good □   Very Good □